ALTERNATIVE AMERICAS

ALTERNATIVE AMERICAS

Mildred J. Loomis

Foreword by Hazel Henderson

A Free Life Editions Book

UNIVERSE BOOKS
New York

Published in the United States of America in 1982
by Universe Books
381 Park Avenue South, New York, N.Y. 10016
© 1980, 1982 Mildred J. Loomis

This is a revised, rewritten, reorganized version of *Decentralism; Where It Came From; Where Is It Going?*, which was issued in a limited edition by The School of Living Press, 1980.

82 83 84 85 /10 9 8 7 6 5 4 3 2 1

Printed in the United States of America

Library of Congress Cataloging in Publication Data

Loomis, Mildred J.
    Alternative Americas.

    Rev. ed. of: Decentralism.
    Bibliography: p.
    Includes index.
    1. Decentralization in government—United States.
I. Title.
JS341.L66 1982   353'.073   81-19775
ISBN 0-87663-375-0   AACR2
ISBN 0-87663-567-2 (pbk.)

Contents

Foreword

THIS FASCINATING REPORT of decentralist thought and action provides indispensable grounding for today's futurists and New Age activists in America. It is an important clarification of the philosophies of anarchism and mutual aid, and their roots in private property. We are shown how the perversion of private property rights for the *individual* led to the monstrous inequities that allowed multinational corporations to masquerade under this protection, as "individual persons" under law. This has led to today's confusion over property rights, which no longer distinguish between the necessary inviolability of individual property rights needed to assure personal autonomy and self-reliance, self-respect, and self-motivation, and the endless accumulation of property by corporations and institutions to the point where they have the power to press and disenfranchise individuals and smaller groups.

This remarkable book helps us to see today's resurgence of co-ops, neighborhood revival, community economic reconstruction, and land trusts in the context of past efforts. By so doing, it helps demonstrate the irrelevance of old political labels, whether they be Republican or Democrat, Liberal or Conservative, capitalist or socialist. Decentralism is one of the keys to understanding the new politics of our time, and how some of the most interesting contemporary figures, from Jimmy Carter to Jerry Brown of California, can be interpreted.

The emerging politics of "small is beautiful" springs from a tradition as old as our nation's founding; from Thomas Jefferson to Ezra Heywood, William B. Greene, J.K. Ingalls, Henry George, and Josiah Warren in the 19th century, to economic and land reformers Ralph Borsodi, Stuart Chase, Elton Mayo, Scott Nearing, and other decentralists of this century, to today's convergence of apparent polar opposites and new groups of strange bedfellows, such as the Libertarians, appropriate technology innovators, small-business people, ecology activists, holistic health-care promoters, advocates of states' rights and consumer protection, together with new labor unions for farm and household workers, advocates of worker-ownership of businesses and neighborhood economic development.

7

This is an invaluable book for those who wish to interpret the new politics of reconceptualization. It documents the earlier experiments and theories of decentralism, and highlights for me the reason that they were overwhelmed by the rising tide of industrialism. That faulty logic was canceled by the cornucopia of resources which earlier, smaller populations could exploit for two centuries before the social bills began coming due. The early decentralists with their more profound ecological and social logic battled the tide and left us their precious legacy, ready for today's New Age decentralists to apply successfully in the receding backwash of the now-exhausted Industrial Era.

Reading Mildred Loomis will ensure that we waste no time reinventing wheels.

Hazel Henderson

Prologue

A KIND OF negativism prevails in America today. People view the 1980s with questions, confusion, and apathy. Generally, it's recognized that the United States is at an ecological low. Farmers mine the soil, and miners rip up the land, leaving it open and unhealed. Forests are removed. Factories pour gases into the air and wastes into the lakes and rivers and oceans. Constantly extended concrete and plastic jungles leave decaying cities with rejected industrial sectors. And the response is blah—masses of people embedded in the 9-to-5 routine, attending mostly to their evening TV and weekend paychecks. The "public" indifferently calls it progress.

In this strange bubbling and simmering America, many individuals have joined groups to develop an alternative style to the "American dream." Conservatives confirm—but not too confidently—faith in competition, profit, and the two-party system. Libertarians discuss and publish the theses of F. A. Hayek, Ludwig von Mises, and Murray Rothbard. Others follow the land reform of Thomas Jefferson and Henry George. Marxists, anarchists, and pacifists similarly pursue their own theories and goals. Still others develop cooperatives and go back to the land.

All of these groups have important things to say and do. But they all suffer from a singlemindedness that is no longer appropriate. What is needed is a holistic solution to the problems facing America today.

The Native Americans

It behooves us to start by looking to the heart of Native Americanism. Native Americans have a special—holistic—way of thinking about the universe and a way of living that results from that philosophy. They supply a depth and challenge too easily neglected as a result of the stereotypes of history and their "isolation," plus the ethnocentricity of European culture.

The essence of the native viewpoint is stated in *Black Elk Speaks:*

> All creation is sacred. Every dawn is a holy event. Their light comes from your Father and the two-leggeds and all the other

people who stand upon this earth are sacred and treated as
such.
The story of all life is old and good to tell, we two-leggeds
sharing in it with the four-leggeds, and the winds of the air
and all green things; all are children of one mother, and their
father is one Spirit. Is not the sky a father and the earth a
mother, and are not all living things with feet or wings or
roots their children?
For us Indians, there is just the Sacred Pipe, the Earth we sit
on, and the open sky. The Spirit is everywhere, showing itself
through an animal, a bird, some tree and hills. Sometimes it
speaks from the Badlands, from a stone, from the water.
If this earth should ever be destroyed, it will be by desire, by
the lust of self-gratification, by greed for the green frog-skin
[money], by people who are mindful only of their own self,
forgetting about the wants of others.
We Indians must show how to live with our brothers, not use
them or maim them. With this Pipe, which is a living part of
the Earth, we cannot harm any part of her without hurting
ourselves. Through this Pipe, we can make peace with our
greatest enemy who dwells deep within ourselves.

Simple ideas with profound implications, raising the question, how
must life be lived if all living things are relatives, brothers and sisters of
the same parent, this Mother Earth?

Interrelated oneness of living is Native Americanism. Yet this nature-
based integral living was overrun and, at least temporarily, overcome by
Europeanism—a philosophy and culture much its opposite: messianic,
authoritarian, materialistic, lacking in humanistic and spiritual values.

How distorted the history and sociology textbook record! Most people
carry the image of courageous emigrants fleeing European chauvinism,
monarchy, exploitation, and materialism to establish a free world on a
"new continent"—America, Land of the Free!

But America was free long before the Europeans arrived, free because of
the way of life that the native peoples had established. In reality, the
Europeans may have found freedom here, but they reestablished here the
same exploitative factors that they fled in Europe. America became, alas,
a base for, and in many cases a replica of, the European tendencies they
hoped to abandon. Some of the consequences of European culture, alien
to Native Americanism, which were established by Europeans and now
dominate 20th-century America have been listed by Jack D. Forbes, a
Native American educator at the University of California at Davis:

(1) the idea that any human being can "own" another living

creature or "own" the earth, the sky, the water, or any natural thing;

(2)   the idea that any human has the right to live off the labor of another human, or off the lives of nonhumans;

(3)   the idea that human beings and other living things, including the earth, can be used as means without regard to the rights and dignity of individual humans, animals, and plants;

(4)   the idea that those who control wealth should be able to determine what is printed, what is seen, and what is heard;

(5)   the idea that the state has a right to know and control what its citizens are thinking, saying, or doing in their private lives;

(6)   the idea that seeking and gaining material wealth and a high standard of living is the most important human activity;

(7)   the idea that slogans of religious or ethical piety can actually replace day-to-day ethical living;

(8)   the general prevalence of arrogance and chauvinism expressed by and granted to persons and ideas of European derivation;

(9)   the messianic mania—the desire to force or high-pressure other people into conforming to the views of some "religious" or political secular unit.

This does not exhaust the Europeanism of America. Forbes lists nineteen others in the Spring 1974 issue of *Akwesasne Notes*, showing how overwhelmingly the "America" of the 1600s–1800s was ideologically, spiritually, historically, and genealogically "Europeanized." Europeans coming to America refused to be Americanized or "naturalized." They wrote, colonized, and developed schools in which the central theme was European. It is difficult not to conclude that virtually every major problem faced in North America today, virtually every kind of unethical behavior, and every threat to individual dignity, freedom, and self-development, has a European origin.

Community, democracy, appropriate technology, natural foods, holistic medicine, anti-statism were born in Native American villages, ranging from north to south and east to west. True, one can point out faults and problems, but only in America, as compared with the Europe of 1500–1700, were any truly free human societies in existence. And they were not products of any "New Age." They had, so far as is known, been growing and developing for thousands of years.

This book is a record of some political, economic, and sociological efforts at freedom and a good life in America. In watching and evaluating them, we do well to note how they deal with and correct the nine serious charges and deposits from Europeanism. We may find among native peoples the best examples of how to live in the 21st century.

1

America's Revolutions

IN ADDITION TO the decentralist life-style of the native people of the Americas—or even perhaps *because* of their example—Europeans on this continent have responded to and followed rebels and revolutionaries for much of their 350-year history here. There have been three revolutions in the ongoing struggle between authority and liberty. Each one has promoted decentralism.

Revolution I: Political

The first comers to Virginia and Massachusetts in the 1600s were resisting and fleeing from religious, economic, and political controls they had known in Europe. In their new country, their hosts were not oppressive, and they enjoyed freedom. They built homes on the land with the land's materials. They developed communities and towns. Separated from their foreign rulers by distance and oceans, with ample land in America, their freedom seemed guaranteed. They were little troubled by "colonial status" in the first hundred years, until excise and other taxes levied by British heads of government became burdensome.

Then, stirred and guided by people such as Tom Paine, the colonists revolutionized their thinking. They would *form* their *own* government; they would write out their *own* rights to free speech, free press, free assembly, and form a constitution to outline the *limited* duties of their elected officials! They declared their independence from King George, dumped taxed tea into Boston Harbor to symbolize rejection of unwanted authority, and defended themselves with bullets against the British Army. These shots were heard round the world. As the thirteen colonies separated from England's monarch, their Declaration of Independence and Constitution of the United States of America gave citizens a cherished voice in government.

"Liberty," the people said, "has been won!" In song and prose, in books and history, this was repeated in the following years, until everyone, in and outside the United States, believed that Americans were freed.

And so they were in a political sense—more free than before their Revolution of Independence. Now they voted and helped form laws to govern themselves. They elected delegates to legislative bodies to represent them. They decided the size and duties of their government—the one agency to which they granted the legal power to use coercion on them. They hoped they would forever restrain this legal power to the enforcement of their human rights, and to the protection from those who would harm their person or property.

Revolution II: Industrial

Having attained their "freedom," Americans turned their muscle, zest, and intelligence to their second revolution—farming the land, producing food, manufacturing and distributing goods, creating money and banks, exporting and importing materials.

New machines and processes were invented. Crops flowed in from fertile farms: corn, wheat, meat, milk, vegetables, fruit, cotton, and tobacco. Coal and metals were mined, oil drilled, ores smelted, brick and pottery fired. Miles of rails were laid. Trains and ships transported American goods around the globe. The land of the free was spearheading its second revolution—a technological and industrial revolution.

Millions of immigrants came. They were told it was the land of inexhaustible resources—forever-productive soil, forests, mines. As the ambitious and oppressed of Europe arrived, businesses flourished, cities grew, and wealth piled up.

Undergirding America's second revolution were the spiritual values of Calvinism, Puritanism, and the Protestant ethic. Sloth was a sin, work a virtue. Everything sustained an unquestioned faith in mass-factory techniques. Given a seemingly boundless Earth, imaginative minds, and ever more people, no end was in sight or imagined for the new Industrial Age.

Yet ghettoes appeared in the cities, slums and shanties in the countryside. Workers sweated out long days in hot foundries, endured tiresome hours at factory benches, grumbled at sunup-to-sundown work on wheat and cotton farms. Economic depressions, bank failures, and panics upset each decade. Mortgaged farms were foreclosed; urban workers were thrown out of work. They protested, besieging employers for jobs, pressuring factory owners for higher wages. Labor and capital were at loggerheads.

Revolution III: Moral and Economic

By the middle of the 1800s came a crucial test of the American Way. The country had developed into three sections—each with a separate economy, with a class that controlled the economics also controlling the politics. Industry and finance dominated the Northeast. The planters of cotton, sugar, and tobacco dominated the South. The diversified farmers had the West. The agrarian West sold its products to the financial Northeast. The plantation owners of the South, relying on African men and women as slaves (i.e., property), preferred to be left alone.

By 1860, the economic rivalry between the North and the South brought on the Civil War, with slavery a secondary but basic issue. The political Constitutional Union Party urged national unity; the Republicans nominated Abraham Lincoln to unite the major groups. Southern leaders urged secession or withdrawal from the Union if Lincoln were elected. When that happened, South Carolina, followed by six others and later five more states, withdrew and established the Southern Confederacy. Four years of bloody war followed before the national government was restored.

In 1863, President Lincoln proclaimed it illegal to treat human beings as property. Slavery was abolished. A third and moral revolution—with economic roots—had been achieved.

In the following half-century, business, industry, and technology expanded further, pushing toward the unquestioned goal of more production, an ever-expanding economy, endless growth. Paper money, centralized banking, the invention of the airplane, and belt-line mass production greatly facilitated what was proudly acclaimed as "progress." Now America was geared not only to an ever-higher standard of living for its own people, but also to feed the hungry of the rest of the world. More and more must be produced. Everyone must work harder. Surpluses piled high.

Industry and industrialism—meaning everybody—grew more and more dependent on expansion and increased production of material goods. Of material goods, along with people's desire for them, so the argument went, there was no end. The Siamese twins, technology and industrialism, brought ever-higher material standards of living. And a higher standard of material living was, in everyone's thinking, the chief, if not the only, component of progress. The almost unanimous conclusion at the turn of the century, and continuing through the 1930s and 1940s, was that progress would insure the good life for everyone.

Perceptive observers, nonetheless, were disquieted with the underlying trend in American history. Industrial, financial, occupational, social, political, and educational affairs had all proceeded in the same direction. All had used the same method—centralization. All were motivated by much the same value system—that happiness lay in the proliferation of material things.

Centralization had proceeded in seven specific areas: (1) production, (2) ownership, (3) control, (4) education, (5) communication, (6) government, and (7) population. To recognize these centralizations, to understand their nature, to evaluate their results in human and spiritual terms, is to see the need for a fourth revolution in American affairs.

2

America's Centralizations

Centralization of Production

OF THE SEVEN centralizations, the most important is the change from small-scale production to large factory production. It is important because the powerful forces struggling for dominance—capitalists and Marxists—both assume the greater efficiency of large-scale production in all things over small-scale production.

Capitalism was launched on its conquering career by acceptance of Adam Smith's idea of centralization in factories, along with the efficiency of unending division of labor. Karl Marx based his idea of "scientific" socialism upon it. Every financier and every advocate of government and economic planning postulated their programs on not only the efficiency of Industrialism but on its inevitability and desirability. All kinds of centralization were considered progressive largely because it was *assumed* that centralized factories were the only efficient means of production.

At the beginning of the 19th century, both agricultural and mechanical production were carried on in farms, shops, and small plants. Mills located on streams, driven by waterpower, kept production localized and in many places. With the coming of the steam engine, production shifted to fewer factories, where power was supplied by boilers and steam engines. Larger and larger units were constructed around the boilers, fueled by coal. Lumber was cut, ores smelted, steel produced in huge mills. People gathered to live nearby to work and produce in factories.

In 1850, 468 iron works and steel mills supplied annually an average of $43,000 per plant to serve 23 million people. Ninety years later, in 1940, 334 steel mills produced an average of $10,000,000 worth of steel per plant for 132 millions of people. With the forming of the U.S. Steel Corporation in 1901, that industry became centralized in Pittsburgh and nearby centers.

A similar growth and centralization occurred in cotton goods, woolen clothing, farm implements and machinery. Whereas shoes were formerly made by custom shoemakers and cloth was woven by local weavers, in the late 1800s and early 1900s shoes and cloth came to be manufactured in large factories and mills in a few favorably located cities.

In the 1850s, grist mills ground flour and meal in every community. Every farm and region raised its own grain. After 1875, millers were responding with large-scale production of refined and bleached white flour processed in huge centralized mills. Growing of wheat was shifted from many small farms to giant farms in Kansas and other western states.

By 1930, the production of food, clothing, furnishings, and machinery had moved into large centers. The largest industry then—manufacturing of automobiles—dominated Detroit. Increasingly, modern industry put production first and human beings second.

Centralization of Ownership—Proletarianism

Companion to centralization of place and production in factories was the centralization of ownership. Prior to 1875, businessmen had largely owned their own means of production. Farmers owned and operated their own farms; retailers owned and ran their own stores; manufacturers owned and managed their own factories. A hundred years later, ownership had been largely centralized.

From 1825 to 1920, the percentage of farms operated by their owners had been cut in half, declining about 4% per year. By 1970, three-fourths of the land was owned by persons other than those who lived on it and cultivated it.

The share of the national wealth held by the richest 1% of the people in the United States is revealing—about 90% of all trust funds and 50% of all corporation stocks are owned by the richest 1%. What was stated in 1941 by the Temporary National Economic Committee is even more true today: "The wealth and income of the country is owned by a few corporations, which in turn are owned by an infinitesimally small number of people. The profits from these corporations go to a very small group, with the result that the opportunities for new enterprises, whether corporate or individual, are constantly restricted."

Several factors influenced the centralization of ownership. One was the support of thinkers, economists, and leaders. Robert S. Brookings of the Brookings Institute voiced a typical attitude and program:

> The best means of hastening the present slow and harrowing process of agricultural regimentation is by forming agricultural corporations which will accomplish in organization and management what big business has accomplished for industry. Following the method in the U.S. Steel Corporation, the most efficient farms (which as now operated are worth less than nothing) would be paid for in safe bonds of the agricultural corporation with some regard for their potential value. . . . The efficient managers would become department managers of the corporation. These corporations would combine all the advantages claimed by Campbell and Ford for large-unit farming, with the additional advantages of efficient management. They would greatly reduce the cost of farming. Their securities would eventually become one of the most extensive and safe investments for our people.

This outright centralist philosophy and method was furthered by World War II. Small farmers and businessmen in every line of enterprise were crushed out by the thousands. War contracts helped centralize the business of the nation in its large corporations.

Centralizing ownership of land, property, and factories into fewer and fewer hands meant transforming individual owners into wage- and salary-earners, totally dependent upon others for their employment and livelihood. Since the 1930s, the American middle class has been educated and conditioned to acquire insurance and, if possible, enough securities to live comfortably in old age. The masses of American workers were encouraged to become dependent upon labor unions and government social security. The masses are no longer, even in theory, supposed to make themselves independent by acquiring property. They are not even expected to save enough (in bank deposits, life insurance, or investments) to meet the hazards of life and the inabilities of old age. Instead, they are trained to turn to an elaborate government social security system to deal with all life's events.

In effect, classical capitalism, with its emphasis on the widespread ownership of property and exchange via the free market has changed into absentee or finance capitalism, rapidly tending toward state capitalism. While centralists validate their goals and methods in terms of "increased efficiency," both leaders and the masses are dismayed with the current results of rapid inflation and rising unemployment.

Centralization of Control

Ownership of a building may be a fact; ownership of bonds or shares of stock may be but fiction or the "shell" of a fact. Control, however, is decidedly a fact. To be able to say "I control" is to say "I have the power that ownership implies." Owners of securities may say, "I own" without being able to say, "I control." They have merely a legal token of ownership.

Corporations make it possible for some people to control property without ownership, and for others, ownership without control. In the U.S. Steel Corporation, a handful of financiers control but do not own its assets. Two hundred thousand stockholders own, but do not control, those assets. Other millions of indirect owners—bondholders, insurance policy holders, depositors in banks—whose savings the corporation invests, have even less control.

The corporation itself holds, in a kind of "trust," vast properties—land and mines, railroads and ships, factories and steel plants, coal, ore, steel, finished products and supplies of all kinds. In legal theory, the ultimate ownership of all this "property" belongs to the stockholders who are assured in annual reports that this is "your" corporation, that the directors and managers represent "you," and that the property is administered for "your" benefit.

In practice, the control of the corporation is centralized in a small group of individuals over whose activities the "owners" (both direct and indirect) have little or no control or influence. Owners may vote in the selection of these controllers, but in reality, controllers of the corporation are virtually a self-perpetuating minority who can administer the property and dispose of its earnings and capital as they think best for their own interests.

The modern business corporation (of which U.S. Steel is one of the most conspicuous) is a device used by promoters (investment bankers) to permit the capitalization of capital (machinery and buildings) and land into capital stock and securities—common and preferred shares—and debentures, bonds, etc. Although this could be a useful function in a complex economy, it fails to be useful today because of the special privileges conferred by law upon incorporators, privileges which are denied to natural persons and partnerships. For instance:

1. Real persons are liable for any debts incurred in their transactions. But by law, the officers and incorporators of corporations are exempt from this obligation. Because of it, corporation officials can expand and take risks. If transactions are unprofitable, they can declare bankruptcy and become exempt from personal liability for the corporation's debts. (Ostensibly, this "special privilege" was granted to encourage the accumulation of large sums for massive business undertakings.)

2. Corporation officials reserve to themselves control and decision-making regarding the stock-shares and deposits made by member-investors.

3. Corporations engage in "stock waterings." They purchase enterprises at one price and capitalize them (sell stock shares) at much higher prices. They manipulate securities on the stock exchange—selling long or short on the basis of inside information.

4. They pay themselves high salaries and bonuses from corporate profits.

5. They pyramid all these activities through "holding corporations."

6. Corporations now "integrate," owning and controlling a whole series of enterprises from production to the consumer. Tenneco can plow fields it owns with its own tractors, fueled with its own oil. It sprays its own crops with its own pesticides and uses its own food additives. It processes its food in its own plants, packages them in containers it has manufactured, and distributes them to its own grocery stores through its own marketing systems. In its 1969 reports, for example, Tenneco listed a gross oil income of $464 million and a taxable oil income of $88.7 million—yet due to federal tax breaks, Tenneco not only paid no taxes on that income, but had a tax credit of $13.3 million. And Tenneco is by no means an exception.

In *The Modern Corporation and Private Property*, Berle and Means stated that 200 of the largest corporations in the U.S. owned $150 billion worth of property. This represented control of 53% of all corporate wealth (other than banking) in the United States, 45% of all business wealth, and 25% of the entire national wealth. In his recent *Corporate Control, Corporate Power*, Edward Herman reassessed the Berle and Means study and concluded that "the corporation has become ever more dominant in economic life." To add to this the savings of people in banks, plus the notes, mortgages, and other collateral given to banks to secure their loans, the centralization of control reaches unfathomable levels.

In fascist Italy and National Socialist Germany, ownership was considered unimportant, but control was quite important. Individuals and corporations were permitted to retain title to their property and to operate their businesses. But control was taken out of their hands by semipublic officials in industry-wide cartels prescribing in detail how the owners were to operate and what they were to do with the proceeds of their "own" enterprises.

In Soviet Russia, individual control was disposed of by forbidding private enterprise altogether and centralizing all ownership and control in the state.

Centralization of Education

When instruction is given by one person to another (parent to child), education is widely decentralized. It is somewhat centralized when a teacher has a class of thirty children. It is further centralized when many small schools are consolidated into one larger one, and further centralized when methods, textbooks, and curriculum are prescribed by state boards or national departments of education. When education's goals (the national cultural pattern) are set in New York, Paris, London, or Moscow, centralization is almost complete. When this last process is made compulsory by law, the ultimate in centralization of education is reached.

The result is that one can now travel from one end of the enormous U.S. to the other and find uniformity in foods, clothes, stores, newspapers, factories, homes, and cities. Individual, family, local, and regional influences that conflict with accepted standards are eliminated.

When people believe that progress is the purpose for which human beings should live, and if progress is identified with the expansion of industrialism, then the whole population must be taught to want the things and live the life that centralized industry alone can produce and provide. What economists call human wants (and advertisers call consumer demand) must be standardized until everybody wants the standardized products of industry and is willing to live the standardized life of an industrial population.

Individuals must be taught, and retaught, with every change in fashion and in technology, to want what industry produces for them. Leaders of industry must concern themselves with both juvenile and adult education. Industry can ill afford to permit any institution to prefer other values than the material values that it alone is capable of supplying. Religion with emphasis on other-worldly values must be neutralized. Patriotism and conservation of civic values must be tempered. Education from the kindergarten to the university must forgo any desire to teach the truth—it must concentrate on preparing the young for life in industrialized society. Industry must take the initiative. In America, its specific device for standardization is advertising and selling.

A whole population cannot be brought to a single classroom for indoctrination. But "education" in the way of advertisements can be taken to the people—to reach the old and young, literate and illiterate, rich and poor, urban and rural. The only useful method is one that produces results—creates demand for the products of specific manufacturers. The largest single group of individuals "teaching" in America are the salesmen and distributors of the products of American industry. Their role is shown by considering that the total sum expended for schooling at all levels plus that spent by religious bodies is only a small percentage of the sum spent on advertising and selling.

According to the *Sales Manager's Handbook*, more than four times is spent on advertising and selling than is spent on the nation's entire school system. Thus parents, teachers, and ministers work in a world saturated by advertising and selling—by those who persuade the public to do what is industrially profitable, and to want what furthers material progress.

Advertisers teach and influence human wants from birth to death. Baby foods are sold to mothers who have been taught by advertisers to substitute them for breast-feeding. Ceremonies surrounding death reflect what is taught by modern casket and funeral industries. No bizarre method or extreme cost deters advertisers from influencing thousands of human wants.

The Media's Part in Centralized Education

For their daily news, most Americans read newspapers, turn on a house or car radio, and sit for hours before The Tube. As with the supermarket or the auto industries, the print and electronic media are being increasingly centralized. Today, most newspapers belong to one of the 167 newspaper chains, now absorbing 50 to 60 papers a year. In 1980, four such chains predominated, raising questions of monopoly ownership, concentrated power, and the deeper question of free speech and how people get news and facts to inform their decisions.

Gannett is the largest chain, owning 78 dailies and working to control an even 100. It now reaches 3 million readers daily—more than the combined daily audience of *The New York Times*, *Los Angeles Times*, and the *Washington Post*. In 1906, F. E. Gannett, a farmer's son, climbed to the editorship of the Ithaca, N.Y., *Daily News*. He bought a nearby newspaper, and in 51 years acquired 30 more and a string of radio and television stations. After his death, the Gannett company went public, increasing both readers and earnings.

The Gannett chain has stiff competition from Knight-Ridder, the owner of 36 dailies, with a circulation of 3.5 million, operating large city dailies—the *Miami Herald*, the *Philadelphia Inquirer*, and the *Detroit Free Press*.

The Newhouse combine, the personal preserve of Samuel I. Newhouse, is known as "the money factory." It publishes 29 small papers (3,281,000 combined circulation) in addition to some magazines (*Vogue*, *Mademoiselle*, *House and Garden*, *Glamour*).

The Tribune Company is the owner of the *Chicago Tribune*, the *New York Daily News*, and seven other dailies (3.1 million circulation). It was described as "a mighty fortress and bulwark of conservatism" by N. R. Kleinfield in the *New York Times Magazine* (9 April 1979). Recently the company has become an aggressive acquirer of papers that do not have competition in cities in which they are located.

Other large chains include Scripps-Howard, Dow Jones and Co., the Hearst Corporation, Times-Mirror, and, of course, the New York Times Company. And as all of these chains grow, readers have less choice. Papers begin to look and read alike.

Where does this leave the readers of newspapers? What about the people's right to know? It all brings up the matter of control. Most large groups claim they grant local autonomy. But conferences are held frequently to exchange ideas and, some say, to exercise control over policy. All publish newspapers whose main purpose is to make a profit.

As the newspaper and other media chains enlarge, the specter of monopoly looms. Said Representative Morris Udall, Democrat from Arizona, "I really shudder to see the day when you have four or five organizations with a hammerlock on what Americans read. . . . The day may come when such leaders hunger for political power. It could be used."

Centralization of Government

The essence of society is *people;* of nation, *territory;* of government, *coercion.* The U.S. government in Washington, democratic as it is supposed to be, is not the people in the United States; nor is it the rich land between the oceans, nor is it a mystical national entity supposed to combine both land and people. Government is that group of officials distinguished by the fact that they and only they have the legal right to exercise authority over the territory and use coercion on the people within its boundaries.

Centralization of government means (1) shifting activities from local officials to national officials, (2) increasing the number of public officials of all kinds, and (3) actually increasing legal coercion in dealing with problems people face. Since the 1930s, the federal government has taken over six types of activities—sometimes to take advantage of federal "efficiency," to assure equalization of public service throughout the country, or to deal with a national emergency. In any case, individuals have less control over their own lives.

The six nationalized activities include:

1. *Political.* In America, nationalization does not abolish state and local officials—local ones continue to perform to a lesser extent. Some political activities once considered primarily state and local and now recognized as national are law enforcement, construction of public improvements; regulation of banks, railroads, exchanges, corporations, etc.; public relief; social security; controlling labor relations. Whereas in 1920 there were 156 federal bureaus, in 1977 there were over 12,000. One hears less and less of "states' rights" and "local autonomy."

2. *Social.* Activities once performed by charitable and philanthropic organizations, by professional and trade associations, by labor unions, by private, school, library, museum, and similar institutions, are now done by federal bureaus.

3. *Individual.* People no longer look to themselves to obtain employment, but to government. Recreational facilities are not provided by individual and family action, but by the "public." Even vital needs cease to be privately provided, as the government provides housing, schools, child care, homes for the aged, and school lunches. With total centralization, as in Soviet Russia, all individual activities become

nationalized and public officials provide facilities for work, play and rest. Thus public officials inescapably prescribe what all individuals shall do.

4. *Ownership of property.* Government administration and ownership of property begin reasonably enough with the regulation of banks, railroads, power companies, public utilities, mining, forestry, and other natural resources. But soon the difference between public and private property is ignored, and regulation changes to intervention by public officials into the operation of private enterprises. This goes further into government ownership of whole industries—banking and mining in Britain, and in Soviet Russia the nationalization of all industries.

5. *Medical services.* The distinction between public and private health is important. Logic supports the use of governmental coercion to deal with epidemics, infectious disease, to enforce quarantine, protect water supply, inspect restaurants. But government goes further into private health by (1) licensing physicians, (2) employing physicians in government health services and hospitals, (3) granting workmen's compensation, and (4) ending with the socialization of all medicine. With total nationalization, not only medicine, but also health, becomes a matter of national and official concern and control, not individual concern.

6. *Education.* Nationalization of the school system begins with the idea that voters must be intelligent in order to select wise officials—hence the education of the young is a civic concern. Everyone is compelled to support schools that every child must attend. Schools, originally, were private, and then came to be established and controlled by local officials and boards. On the plea of efficiency, their control is shifted to state supervisors and departments. On the plea of equalizing educational opportunities, control shifts to the national government.

Nationalization of education seems to prevent the communication of ideas that have not been officially approved. Anything anti-official is suppressed. The official doctrines and propaganda are imposed on everybody. In addition, to the extent that government officials license halls and eating places, control the use of the post office, telephone, and radio, or acquire control of printing and paper, the foundation is laid for disseminating official propaganda and preventing circulation of anti-official sentiments. Only the American belief in free speech and assembly holds censorship somewhat in abeyance.

Comparing population and government employees reveals the extent of nationalization. In 1816, there was one civil servant (including the military) to every 1,336 persons. By 1950, there was one person governmentally employed to every 44 persons in the country, and if armed services and state and local government employees are added in, there was in 1950 one government employee for every four families (16 persons) in the United States.

Centralization of Population

In industrial nations, people have been concentrating on smaller and smaller areas of land, with resulting depopulation of the rural areas, and overpopulation of cities.

In 1970, the U.S. continental area was 3,540,023 square miles, on which lived 203,212,000 people, or an average density of 57 persons per square mile. Of course, 57 persons did not live on every square mile; the density in specific areas gives a truer picture. Nevada had an average density of four persons per square mile; Rhode Island 902, and Ohio 260 persons per square mile.

In cities, of course, the density intensifies. Thus in one square mile of New York City are crowded more people than the whole of New York City's 1800 population.

In 1890, 57% of the total U.S. population lived in strictly rural areas; by 1930, the rural population had declined by one-third, or 36.4%. Each census since then has reported more people moving from rural to urban areas than have returned to the country. In 1975, however, for the first time in history, more people left American cities than entered them to reside there.

By way of these seven centralizations, modern America by the 1980s has reached an epitome of progress and affluence. Concrete and stone are layered, level upon level, until buildings tower a hundred stories or more into the air. Vast cities stretch along both East and West seacoasts. In between, each state is building to match Chicago. Subway tunnels burrow into the earth, and tracks are elevated to transport millions of people speedily between their jobs and their homes. People communicate instantly across continents by telephone, radio, and TV. The quantity age is with us.

3

The Failure of Centralization

IF MODERN PROGRESS is a good goal for which human beings should live, then as people industrialize, urbanize, and centralize, the quality of their lives should also improve. How about quality? Are people more satisfied? Are they happier, surfeited with things, than in an earlier day of simpler living? Has centralization served them well?

To answer these questions, one must have a standard—a criterion—from which to rate and judge life in the modern day. Here I use several tests—economic, ethical, psychological, physiological, and esthetic—by which to test the results of the seven centralizations. I assume, with Ralph Borsodi, that normal human beings are able to, and do, support themselves; that they are able to bear and nurture healthy young, and that both adults and children are physically and mentally healthy; that they do not commit crime; that they enjoy beauty and that their producing/making of things is satisfying and artistic. In brief, normal human beings avoid dependency, disease, degeneracy, delinquency, and decadence. Largely as a result of centralization, however, these five D's have become problems of epidemic proportions.

Dependency

Dependency is the state of those who receive their food, clothing, and shelter from others. Dependency of young children on parents is normal; dependence of healthy adults on others for maintenance is abnormal. Persons earning their maintenance are also dependent if they have no alternative to their employment—if they have no savings or property; if they are subject to arbitrary dismissal by an employer, dictation by union officials, or regimentation by government officials as to hours of work, wages, or salary.

The total of both normal and abnormal dependents includes about one-half of the whole U.S. population. Industrialism and urbanism prevent millions of city children from contributing to self-support. Country children at ten years of age can be almost totally supporting. The number of parasitic and nonproductive persons (and those who have no alternative to being employed by others) is constantly rising, while the self-supporting numbers are constantly declining.

Three trends in modern industrialism raise the number of nonworkers: (1) increasing the age at which children can work, along with extending the years during which children and youth are in school; (2) lowering the age of adults for retirement; (3) urban homes becoming consuming instead of producing units. This last deprives both children and the aging of the productive work they used to perform on country farms and homesteads.

With modern industry has come increasing economic interdependence. Interdependence is good where individuals do not become parasites or lose their alternatives for self-employment.

Industrialism is constantly increasing the number of persons who distribute instead of produce. A hundred years ago, only 3% of the population were distributors. And most of them were merchants and shopkeepers in business for themselves. In the 1980s, 40% are hauling, selling, or advertising goods. In a day of mail-order houses, of department and chainstores, distributors are mostly sales clerks and employees entirely dependent for their livelihoods upon employment by others. An increasing proportion becomes parasitic and dependent. To whatever extent this violates human nature and involves people in frustration, it disposes them to disease, degeneracy, and delinquency.

Delinquency

Delinquency refers not merely to breaches of the law but to acts that violate society's ethical standards. Delinquency refers to habitual behavior where character is involved, not merely to a single or occasional act. Delinquency includes crimes against person or property (assaults and thefts); violation of a people's moral sense (lying); imposition upon rights of others; legal acts of predation ("featherbedding" by unions); legal exploitation (special privilege and monopoly); legal extortion (usury of investment bankers); sexual crimes and misbehavior; and improvidence.

The increase of criminal behavior in the modern world is well known. In *The Criminals We Deserve*, Henry T. F. Rhodes says:

> Mass production is more than industrial technique. We mass-produce criminals too. Modern industrial society has produced the modern slum, the worst of all mass-produced articles. . . . Great wealth has been created, but in the scramble for it, the slum remains. That contradiction is reflected in the mind and heart of the underdog. A great struggle ensues between the modern criminal and modern society. The revolt of the criminal is often a revolt against intolerable conditions.

In *Principles of Criminology*, Edwin Hardin Sutherland shows that the great rise in modern mobility has increased crime. Seaports, resort towns, and those with transient populations have the highest crime rates, which increase with the size of the community. As population has shifted from farms and villages to huge metropolitan centers, crime has become more and more common. The pattern seems to be "the larger the city, the greater the number of crimes." The trend was evident to Sutherland, who said, "As people become more and more industrial, and they devote themselves to acquiring higher and higher standards of living, they depend less on home and family, and organize their lives more and more around social and political institutions. With it, delinquency and crime naturally increase."

Not all crimes are reported or prosecuted. Criminologists assume that of every hundred crimes perpetrated, only five are reported and of them, only two prosecuted. Yet recorded figures show that crime and delinquency continue to increase. White-collar crime—a special, "modern" category of crime—goes unreported even more often. With persistent cries for "law and order," it is clear that criminal behavior in modern society has gotten out of hand.

Disease

Modern medical practice and sanitation have reduced the rate of blindness in America. But they have not reduced the number suffering from poor eyesight. Modern people definitely see less clearly than primitive ones. Similarly, sanitation and inoculation are credited with reduction of infectious diseases—malaria, smallpox, typhoid. Medical technology has made life tolerable—even useful and productive—for many with physical defects or blindness or deafness.

But modern, centralized civilization has produced an ailment peculiarly its own—anomie and alienation. The French sociologist Emile Durkheim maintained that in proportion as an industrial society develops, people suffer from anomie—a restlessness that turns to apathy. In a small society (or society of small groups), life is ordered so that the interests of its members contribute to the group. During infancy and adolescence, an individual sees ahead how he will function when he is adult. This anticipation regulates his thought and action, and culminates in adult satisfaction in being useful and necessary to his group. Since modern life does not supply this training and experience, planlessness and anomie result. Happiness lies beyond present achievement; defeat turns to disillusionment and to disgust with the "futility of endless pursuit."

Degeneration

Moreover, modern life has brought a terrifying increase in physical and mental degeneration—heart trouble, diabetes, muscular dystrophy, cancer, psychopathology, drug addiction, sexual perversion, sterility, and insanity. One in four Americans in the 1980s is developing cancer, and one-third of those will die from it. Stress, devitalized food, isolated sedentary living all contribute to lack of resistance and degenerative disease in modern America. Obviously, some defectives are unavoidable in any population, but in a normal healthy society their percentage would be low, and the rate would not rise. The statistics from a typically modern industrialized area (New York State) show the reverse. The rate of insanity per 100,000 persons increased steadily from 1850 (67.3) to 1880 (183.3) to 1931 (273.0) to 1942 (364.2). Similarly, the number of patients per 100,000 people who are in New York mental hospitals increased from 1889 (260.4) to 1927 (422.5) to 1940 (637.6) to 1970 (2,481)!

Benjamin Malzburg in *Social and Biological Aspects of Mental Disease* said, "Approximately one person out of twenty-two becomes a patient of mental disease during a generation. . . . One out of six [newly born persons] will spend a part of his life in a mental institution. At this rate, by the year 2000, one of every two persons will experience mental disease."

The rate of insanity in cities is twice as high as in rural America.

Mayo's Chicago map plotted for crime showed a similar pattern for insanity—the rate near the Loop was the highest, and the decline was proportional toward the periphery.

Rates for suicide (total escape from living) are equally indicative. Suicides are 50% higher per capita in urban than in rural areas, with the rate on the increase.

Decadence

How satisfying are the work of modern people and the things they produce? How satisfying are their play and leisure activities?

If work is satisfying, it is so because it uses *all* the aspects of the person working—it uses his whole being, his body, mind, and will. A man is making a chair. He uses his mind to design it; his will to decide that it is for his wife's comfort; he carefully chooses his materials and tools. Then he executes it with his hands and muscles. Completed, it is *his* chair. No one gave him a pattern, saying, "Make it like this." No one handed him pine when he knew it should be oak. Only with his own sharp saw and chisel could he make a *good* chair—one that expressed his own *self*; he feels completed, fulfilled, satisfied.

Such integral self-expression is instinctive to human beings, strong in every normal person. Industrial work—factory work—distorts it. People become specialists, only designing, only cutting, only assembling, or only polishing. Too often workers are tenders of machines or punchers of buttons—not so much making things as making money.

Leisure activities are likewise distorted in modern industrial society. Instead of singing or dancing to return refreshed to the work they love (as in more wholesome societies), moderns resort to watching, viewing, and consuming the activities and objects produced by others. They go to the theater, opera, sports arena, and stay glued to the TV to soothe or stimulate jaded nervous systems. Modern man works and plays in ways that degrade his nature. Whatever the origin of humans, they are creatures who know and will and love. Yet cruelty, irresponsibility, and ignorance increase. Such falling away from nature is a degradation and inhuman.

Centralization has not lessened the prevalence of the five D's. On the contrary, there is more dependency, disease, degeneration, delinquency, and decadence. What is clearly and desperately called for, then, is a fourth revolution—a decentralist revolution.

Decentralization is not a turning back of the clock. Through decentralization, independence would replace dependency; honesty and justice would replace delinquency. Health would prevent disease and degeneracy. Creative work and folk art would replace decadent and inhuman activities.

For these desired ends, decentralization would organize production, control, ownership, government, communications, education, and population in smaller, more human units.

Such a trend is apparent as we have moved into the 1980s. The worm is turning. Important groups and wise individuals have contributed to decentralist ends and means in American history. Some have worked significantly and dropped out of sight. Others continue, more or less obscurely. Most of them have been crowded out of school textbooks and hidden from public discussion by the all-conquering centralization of modern times. But hundreds of thousands of people are seeking human alternatives. Thousands of groups are publishing journals, exchanging newsletters, and getting into action over environmental, social, political, energy, and many other issues. Knowledge, support, and guidance are at hand in American decentralist forebears. In the following chapters, I present some of the outstanding leaders and groups who make up America's fourth and decentralist revolution.

These groups include America's early voluntarists or individualist anarchists, headed by Josiah Warren; the land-reformers led by philosopher/economist Henry George; the cooperators first launched by the Rochdale weavers in 1844; and especially the decentralists guided by Ralph Borsodi and the School of Living.

4

Individualists: Replacing Government with Voluntary Action

IN MODERN SOCIETY, people everywhere are born into an area "ruled" by some government. By law, citizens at their maturity become supporting, tax-paying members of that government. Attempts to withdraw, or failure to pay support-taxes, result in imprisonment or fine. Had Americans insisted on Jefferson's view that "government is an evil to be watched like fire," instead of becoming centralists, they would have held government to its one legitimate function of protecting life, liberty and property.

Other Americans have gone even further than Jefferson toward liberty and voluntary action. They have advocated replacing government with voluntarism. I present them first because their comprehensive challenge to centralism surfaced *before* other fourth revolutionaries came on the scene. Their legacy is very important for an understanding of decentralism.

From about 1790 to 1930, America produced a group who believed, taught, and demonstrated that *all* human activities and all organizations should be voluntary—that even defense need not be governmental and coercive. They worked hard to free the economy of monopoly and exploitation in order that crime would be reduced, and the need for defense would fall to a minimum.

Persons holding these beliefs and practices sometimes call themselves "individualist anarchists." Examining the root meaning of "anarchy," we find that "an" means no or none, "archy" means rulership. Thus "anarchy" means no rulership or *enforced* authority. Anarchy does not mean chaos and disorder. Such misunderstanding and misuse of the term stems from the 1886 Haymarket Affair in Chicago, when workers in the McCormick Harvester Corporation were on strike. In a public demonstration supporting the strikers, someone threw a bomb. Several policemen and bystanders were killed. In spite of pleas of innocence, eight anarchists were indicted. Even today, persons who have professed anarchism are not eligible for immigration or entry to the United States.

The terms *anarchist, anarchism,* and *anarchy,* have been used so loosely that their specific meaning of no *enforced* authority has been obscured. Anarchists do, of course, believe in authority, and in leadership, and in organization—all voluntary and unimposed. It is an error to use "anarchy" to mean chaos, or mere hostility to the status quo.

True anarchists hold that individual choice is primary to maturity and responsibility. For this, they hold that private property is essential, that is, for courageous dissident beliefs or actions, a person must be beholden to no one—neither to employer nor group nor government. For such independence, he needs a place of his own, inviolable and private to himself, from which he can produce his own survival, and from which he cannot be excluded for speech or actions that harm no one. To ensure widespread private property, individualist anarchists work to remove all forms of privilege and monopoly that centralize property, ownership, and control into the hands of a few people.

America produced a group of sturdy individualist anarchists who adhered to decentralized local communities, and free association of producers and consumers in urban centers. They abandoned the ideal of an *equalitarian* utopia where everyone was an *economic equal* under pooled property. Instead, they worked for a world of *equity*—a world free of legal privilege and free from legal restrictions to opportunity to work and live. I present below a brief introduction to seven of the most important of these individualist anarchists.

Josiah Warren

First in time and in scope of his efforts was Josiah Warren (1798–1874). A New England musician and inventor, he joined the trek west in 1819 to better his economic condition. He settled in Cincinnati and might have become a wealthy man, had not Robert Owen's cooperative colony at Harmony, Indiana, impressed him with its social reform.

Robert Owen assumed that human nature was a constant, with man's character and behavior resulting from outside environmental forces.

Consequently, desirable conduct would result from good societal influences. In Scotland, Owen had already developed unsurpassed living and working conditions in his factory, and he wanted to extend such in the new continent. From its Rappite owners, Owen purchased the Harmony, Indiana, colony, renamed it New Harmony, and brought in settlers sympathetic to his ideas.

Josiah Warren joined the group and helped draft the Constitution of New Harmony, Community of Equality. But New Harmony was short-lived. Due to Owen's absence on business abroad, and to a basic error in principle, as Warren saw it, New Harmony died out in two years. Warren also blamed its demise on the submergence of the individual within the community. "It appeared that it was nature's own inherent law of diversity that had conquered us," he wrote; "our 'united interests' were directly at war with the individualities of persons and circumstances."

Warren went on his own to experiment with equality of labor—to exchange all labor employed in the production of goods and services equally, hour for hour. On 18 May 1827, he opened a retail store in Cincinnati with $300 worth of groceries and dry goods. He posted the bills of purchase so that all could see what had originally been paid for the goods on sale. A cost price was charged, plus 7% markup for shipping and store overhead. For his own labor, Warren required the purchaser to give him a labor note promising an equal amount of the customer's work. From a large clock, all could see the time spent in exchange. Warren was gratified with the success of "The Time Store," and a few other merchants undertook the plan.

Warren's further goal, however, was to establish a community on voluntary individualist principles. In his *Equitable Commerce* (1847), Warren discarded all varieties of collectivism, paternalism, all political and violent revolutionary action. He defined his individualist stand, the proper reward of labor, emphasized the security of personal property and freedom of the individual. He summed it all up in two slogans: "Sovereignty of the Individual" and "Cost, the Limit of Price."

Warren's solutions dispensed with government other than that of each person over himself. "The only ground upon which human beings can know liberty is that of disconnection and individuality." For Warren, a prerequisite of a self-sufficient society was the decentralization of manufacturing, confined to production for local needs. Warren's chief energies, however, went into forming communities demonstrating his principles.

On 400 acres in Tuscarawas County, Ohio, community members built houses and a sawmill on the labor-for-labor principle. Capital was supplied without interest. In 1834, America had a full-fledged anarchist community long before anything similar was attempted in Europe. But Tuscarawas land was in a low-lying area, subject to malaria. An epidemic spread among the thirty families, and the first equity village was abandoned in 1835.

Warren spent the next ten years on inventions and publishing; his enthusiasm for new experiments continued. In 1842, he opened his second "Time Store" on the outskirts of New Harmony. Again customers exchanged labor for labor, and used the labor-note currency. Resulting price cuts brought customers from a hundred miles around.

In 1847, Warren persuaded some of the Owenites who had been at New Harmony to join him in the cost-price individualist variety of decentralization. In their new community, Utopia on the Ohio River, some one hundred residents built and operated a sawmill, a grist mill, a steam mill, and a carpentry shop, using the labor-exchange ideal, the labor-note currency, and a time store, selling basic merchandise. Warrenism remained there for over a quarter of a century, while Warren's major energies swung to the East.

In New York and Boston, Warren had the intellectual stimulus of other individualists. In 1851, he began another equitist community, Modern Times, on 750 acres on southern Long Island, 40 miles east of New York City. Land was sold to hand-picked settlers (at $20 an acre-lot) who in turn screened later buyers to eliminate those hostile to the cost principle. They built homes of the gravel-lime mixture of the area. Warren erected his house for $120 and later sold it for the same sum.

Warren's concept of individuality put no restraints on personal, religious, or moral practices. That women at Modern Times wore men's clothing and bloomers was a scandal to outsiders, and was the basis for an attack on Modern Times as a center of sexual irregularity. Such charges were unfounded, and when a barrage of innuendo in New York newspapers led Warren to issue a public refutation, Modern Times could no longer continue in pleasant obscurity.

Two members of Modern Times added to the unsavory public image with their social causes. Dr. Thomas L. Nichols deplored the state's sanction of marriage, and Henry Edger, an Englishman, took up the ideas of August Comte that "only society exists—society determines individuals."

Warren nonetheless was satisfied that Modern Times felt little shock from the economic panic of 1857. Unlike the general public, Modern Timers were not affected by the over-issue of currency. Their labor notes were accepted in payment of taxes during the depression that followed the panic.

Crime was never a problem in Modern Times. Lack of disorder and violence in the absence of constituted authority for such a long period is a challenge to those who believe that organized society without a "ruler" is doomed to chaos.

The only "government" Warren proposed was a system of deliberative bodies, approximating courts, consisting of wise older members. These counselors served for the voluntary contributions from those who used their services. The counselors aired the citizen's disputes before all who cared to be present. In case of civil disorder, Warren approved the use of a group trained in *preventative* techniques to use *restraint* in protecting persons or property.

Ezra Heywood

A native of Westminster, Massachusetts, and a graduate of Brown University, Ezra Heywood (1833–93) was vigorously involved in the antislavery movement. Meeting Josiah Warren persuaded him to search for the causes of poverty. Gradually, he gave up belief in political action and formed the New England Labor Reform League to work for "free contracts, free money, free markets, free transit, free land—by discussion, petition, remonstrance and the ballot to establish these articles of faith as a common need and a common right."

Heywood moved to Princeton and established the Cooperative Publishing Company, the center of antistatist publications for over a decade. Its *Declaration of Sentiment of the Reform League* has few equals as an indictment of the existing American society. Land, including all minerals, was to be held as common property; opportunity was open to all individuals to use and occupy such resources during their lifetimes. Tariffs were to be removed. Labor-note currency should circulate in free public markets. The services of railroads, telegraph, and express lines should be provided at cost, resulting from free, open competition among them.

In 1869, Heywood published *Yours or Mine,* showing why *occupancy and use* of land was the only valid title to land. An individual could claim only that land which he actually occupied and used in his own livelihood. Monopoly (ownership permitted by government) and not "society" was responsible for the rise of land values. Absolute ownership of land in excess of its use created inequality of wealth. A second cause was the "exclusive" or monopolized currency. Both rent of land and interest on money, according to Heywood, were nothing but taxes on labor.

> Since money is the common measure of products, and exchanges must be made in the accepted currency, it is apparent that if speculators control this medium, dictating its nature, amount, and value, they are masters of both labor and trade, and can tax us on the chance to do business, and also for the privilege of living.

Heywood assaulted the limited economy (gold and silver) basis of money, and called for a free currency issued by a mutual (cooperative) bank. Anything that had exchangeable value was money. Since property had exchangeable value, property was suitable backing for money.

Heywood established a journal, *The Word,* and it became a catalyst for a group of varied reformers including Josiah Warren, Bronson Alcott, William B. Green, Lysander Spooner, some Owenites, Fourierites, and feminists. *The Word* circulated widely in America, Europe, and South Africa. Heywood taught that "government was a conspiracy of the wealthy for their own interests"; he attacked the possessors of large fortunes, the graduated tax, the abuse of the eight-hour-day law, promoted radical feminist ideas, and opposed legal marriage. Warren and others did not support Heywood in everything, but Heywood was undaunted by criticisms and suggestions.

In 1877, Heywood was charged with circulating obscene material through the mail. Because of his defense of female independence, Heywood was arrested and jailed. A mass meeting of 6,000 people protested. Heywood and friends secured 70,000 signatures to a petition to repeal the Comstock laws. Released, Heywood continued working for "a union of various aspects of the intellectual radical movement" (interrupted by another jail sentence) until his death in 1893. His published works on Josiah Warren and William B. Greene are his best contributions to decentralist history.

William B. Greene

The panic of 1837 with its drastic curtailment of credit stirred widespread concern in economic and financial circles. Banking abuses gave rise to many proposed radical remedies. People generally feared an alliance between big bankers and politicians; they looked for solutions on a local level, by-passing large scale reforms. A drive for centralized banking was meeting opposition in that period. Into this unrest came anarchist ideas, chiefly those of William B. Greene, on money and banking, on which Warren and Heywood had been inconclusive.

Born in Haverhill, Massachusetts, William B. Greene (1810–78) was educated at West Point, took part in a campaign against the Seminoles in Florida, but came to see war as unjust. He prepared for the ministry and wrote religious tracts. His expositions on mutualism in banking began in the Worcester *Palladium* in 1849. Expanded as *Mutual Banking*, it became the most widely reprinted of anarchist publications on finance by an American.

Dr. James Martin, a prominent historian of American anarchism, says,

> A bank in Greene's opinion had only one reason for existing: that of being a place to bring together borrowers, and lenders, regardless of what the particular capital available for lending consisted, and what was wanted by the borrower. The man without tools and raw material was helpless despite any degree of industry, while the owner of such things faced the prospect of watching them deteriorate in the event that laborers desiring them for production purposes could not be found.

Greene saw that banks as then constituted were not acting in the interests of the people of the community. He regarded the free competition among owners of capital as healthful, lowering the rate of interest, and thus guaranteeing to the worker a larger percentage of his production. Once a bank became organized, this process ceased. "In banks, capitalists combine to prevent a fall in the price of money (the commodity they have to offer); legislatures applaud their action and grant them charters to accomplish their purpose more easily."

Greene believed that outside competition with banks would lower the interest rate. He would provide money to borrowers "at cost" as Warren suggested. His remedy for cycles of depressions and money shortage, and his alternative to the economic control of the government-chartered banking fraternity, was the *mutual bank.*

Any person could become a member of the mutual cooperative bank by pledging mortgages to the cooperative on actual property. Upon this, he would be issued bills of exchange amounting to one-half the total value of his property. All members agreed to accept such paper for all payments when presented by fellow members. The member was released from his pledge when his mortgage had been redeemed.

This system was a mutual agreement to monetize values other than gold and silver to one-half the declared valuation of those other values—that is, labor products or property. While Greene agreed with keeping silver as the *standard* of value, he extended the backing (or redemption) of money to commodities. Greene believed such money would escape the evils of both scarcity and excess of supply. It would always be worth its face value in silver dollars, because money would be redeemable at sight only in merchandise and services. Banking paper would be issued on products.

Thus, a person with only his labor to offer could easily borrow capital to engage in productive work, and thus create capital goods of his own. Mutual bank currency would be offered at cost (probably 1% of the amount loaned) but without additional interest. Said Greene:

> Mutualism operates, by its very nature, to render political government, founded on arbitrary force, superfluous. It operates to the decentralization of the political power, and to the transformation of the State by substituting self-government instead of government *ad extra*. In times of economic distress, mutual money would be a bulwark against inflation and deflation—citizens cannot fail disastrously, for the real property is always there, rooted in the ground.

In England in 1878, Greene's death brought to an end the career of the ablest native-born American anarchist writer on finance. Mutual banking and currency, allowing for the monetization of all durable wealth, now became a core of antistatist finance.

J. K. Ingalls

The early life of J. K. Ingalls (1816–96) was similar to that of Heywood and Greene. Born in Swansea, Massachusetts, he became a convinced Quaker, espoused the diet reform of Sylvester Graham, supported the followers of Robert Owen and François Fourier, promoted labor unions, and joined the abolitionists.

In 1845, Ingalls met leading figures in the Land Reform Society and was convinced that the money and property systems rested on "usury in land or ground rent." His interest in restricting the size of landholdings, in one form or another, took precedence thereafter.

In 1849, Ingalls met Josiah Warren and other anarchists. From their ideas, he refined and extended his land reform to occupancy-and-use as the only valid title to land.

Giving up effecting reforms through legislation, Ingalls tried forming a community for a way of life freer of commercialism. In 1849, he planned his "Mutual Township" or "Cooperative Brotherhood." In 1850, he and a group began to work on a site near Parkersburg, West Virginia. Although the community continued until 1865 and beyond, its social ideas tapered off to comfortable living.

Ingalls transferred his efforts to the National Land Reform Association and worked to repeal all laws that granted titles to absentee landholders, restricting protection only to land titles based on personal occupancy and use. He wrote for Heywood's *The Word* and other radical journals. He studied business failures and credit stringency and accepted Greene's Mutual Bank, yet he firmly held that monopolization of the land is the chief source of economic disorder and distress.

In his book, *Social Wealth*, Ingalls advanced four reasons why land should not be subject to permanent tenure sale: (1) it is not a product of human labor; (2) it is limited in amount and unable to react to "demand"; (3) it cannot be removed and transferred; and (4) occupancy ends with the occupant's death. Labor could claim only occupancy of land as base for title and could claim only the land's product for sale. Ingalls deplored issuing of greenbacks by the state. His long struggle for land reform and rejection of political action for attaining it helped firmly establish tenure by occupation and use in anarchist teaching.

Stephen Pearl Andrews

Stephen Pearl Andrews (1812–80), born in Templeton, Massachusetts, took part in all phases of native anarchism. As a young lawyer in Texas, he was mobbed for his abolitionist activity. He went to London to seek a British loan for Texas to purchase and release slaves, but did not succeed.

Back in America, Andrews wrote articles in support of cooperation and Fourierism. He met Josiah Warren in 1848 and saw the advantage of Warren's approach over "combination of interests." Andrews then restated Warren's *Equitable Commerce* in a smooth and finished document, *The Science of Society*, declaring that individual sovereignty, free voluntary association, and a cost basis of price were immutable principles. Conformity with them produces harmony in the affairs of mankind, he wrote; departure from them, confusion.

Stephen Pearl Andrews had access to columns in the *New York Tribune* to discuss Warren's principles. There he wrote:

> The most stupendous mistake that this world of ours has ever made is that of erecting an abstraction, the State, the Church, Public Morality according to some accepted standard . . . into a real personality, and making it paramount to the will and happiness of the individual. . . . Give up . . . the search after the remedy for the evils of government in more government. The road lies just the other way—toward individuality and freedom from all government. . . . Nature made individuals, not nations; and while nations exist at all, the liberties of the individual must perish.

Andrews admitted two obstacles to completely dispensing with government—the magnitude of combined interests in which human society was already involved, and the need for an authority somewhere to restrain encroachments. Yet he maintained his interest in natural government and natural organization—that is, the self-election or spontaneous recognition of leaders, coupled with the continuous freedom to revolt on the part of the subjects.

In spite of his commitment to abolition, Andrews found the freedom of the individual of more importance than that of the southern states, saying, "The scientific and harmonious adjustment of capital to labor, of employee to employer, will remain long after the issue of Slavery is dead." Andrews also supported a self-regulating system of currency and banking, based directly on labor.

An English leader declared that Andrews was "probably the most intellectual man on the planet," and Benjamin Tucker, editor of *Liberty*, said "Andrews' *Science of Society* was the ablest English book ever written in defense of Anarchist principles."

Lysander Spooner

Lysander Spooner (1808–87) left his father's farm in Athol, Massachusetts, at age 25, to work in Worcester's registry of deeds and to study law under two noted jurists. He practiced for seven years in Ohio, and wrote his unorthodox *Deist's Reply to Alleged Supernatural Evidences in Christianity*. He supported opposition to supernal authority as well as to the state.

The panic of 1837 opened his eyes to the exploitative nature of banking by private corporations and the increasing complication from political and governmental bodies. In his *Constitutional Law Relative to Credit, Currency, and Banking,* he said, "to issue bills of credit and promissory notes for the payment of money is as much a natural right as to manufacture cotton."

The creation of compulsory legal tender, according to Spooner, was an infringement of the constitutional clause upholding the obligation of contracts. The making of a contract, he said, was an act of *real persons,* and should be restricted to such persons. "The idea of a joint, incorporeal being (i.e., corporation or government) made up of several real persons, is nothing but fiction." When profits accrued from banking operations, the individuals in whose names the chartering had taken place appeared to collect. Yet the "heads of corporations" were protected from loss. Bank charters gave individuals two advantages—"one favorable to making contracts, the other favorable to avoiding the responsibility of them."

In 1844, Spooner organized the private American Letter Mail Company, delivering mail between Boston, New York, Philadelphia, and Baltimore more cheaply and expeditiously than the government's service. Rather than improving public service and competing with Spooner's private service, Congressional action was to "put private mail service out of business." Spooner replied that Article I, Section 8 of the U.S. Constitution gave Congress the right to establish its post office, but "it did not *prohibit* individuals from doing the same." The power to establish and the power to prohibit were two distinct and separate powers.

Spooner also showed that government monopoly of mail led to excluding such materials as it wished. Limiting circulation of mail amounted to infringement on printing and selling material as well. Spooner objected to an exclusive national system of mails on both moral and economic grounds. Congress set up stiff fines for carrying of mails by any other than the government postal system, and Spooner's independent mail companies were virtually eliminated in 1845.

Spooner published other pamphlets, and in 1861 he proposed a decentralized banking system similar to Greene's. It held that currency should represent an invested dollar rather than a gold or silver one and that mortgages on fixed property should be the backing of money. Mortgages for redemption were always to be ample and open to public inspection. Those who used the currency should know by what and by whom it was backed. In this way, a democratic, sound, and abundant currency with a low interest rate would be guaranteed by competition, limited only by the amount of real property, which was more plentiful than gold and silver.

Spooner introduced his bank project in 1864, and again in 1873, but did not succeed in getting it past banking and governmental opposition. His insistence that congressional power to coin and regulate money did not include the power to make its use mandatory, and that debtors were free to pay debts in wheat, corn, hay, iron, wool, cotton, beef, or anything they choose, opened up ideas to be implemented later by others.

Through a long series of political writings, Lysander Spooner went on to unalloyed antistatism. Through these run the concepts of natural law, natural justice, and natural rights, which led him to denounce all man-made government as superfluous. In *No Treason, No. VI*, Spooner questioned the validity of the U.S. Constitution itself. He held that signers of the U.S. Constitution had no power to contract for others than themselves in any matter. To maintain that a group of men might make political agreement binding on future generations was no more valid than to believe that they had power to make business or marriage contracts mandatory on future persons. Constitutional signers could pledge their support no longer than their own life span. The Constitution was the work of, and pledged the support of, only those who signed it.

In *Trial by Jury*, Spooner showed his distrust of government. He recommended that judges presiding over jury trials be elected by the people, and not appointed by government officials. From Spooner also comes the choosing of jurors from the names in a box.

In *No Treason* (1876), Spooner attacked the conduct of the Civil War, the Republican Party, and the whole structure of political democracy. He held that treason was conduct contrary to what had been pledged. Open revolt could not be treason unless prior consent could be proved. He contended that neither voting nor payment of taxes was valid evidence of either support or attachment to the Constitution.

Benjamin R. Tucker

It remained for Benjamin R. Tucker (1854–1939) and his journal, *Liberty*, to bring individualist anarchism into the 20th century. Born in New Bedford, Massachusetts, the son of radical Unitarians in comfortable circumstances, he attended a local Friends Academy. He spent three years at the Massachusetts Institute of Technology. Tucker became a supporter of Prohibition, women's suffrage, the eight-hour day, and religious radicalism. Still too young to vote, he formed a political discussion club in New Bedford. In 1872, he met Josiah Warren and William B. Greene, and began a life-long career as an antistatist thinker. Young Tucker's articles in The Word led to his association with its editor, Ezra Heywood. Through that journal, Tucker became familiar with Warren's labor exchange and "Cost, the Limit of Price"; with Greene's mutual bank; with J. K. Ingalls's land occupancy-and-use; with Spooner's no-government ideas; and with Heywood's literary productions.

Tucker became part of Heywood's staff on The Word, and in 1874 he made the first of several trips to Europe to study the French anarchist, Pierre Joseph Proudhon. On 8 August 1875, Tucker announced his refusal to pay the poll tax in Princeton, Massachusetts, the home of Heywood. He was jailed but soon released when an unknown friend paid his tax. Despite his long period of literary attack, this was Tucker's only clash with the machinery of the state.

Of more importance was the publication of Tucker's translation of Proudhon's 500-page What Is Property? For Tucker, Proudhon was the "profoundest political philosopher who ever lived." At age 21, Tucker was acknowledged a literary power among America's outstanding voluntarists, all older than he.

Because Heywood gave too much space in The Word to "love reform rather than labor reform," and wanting to further explore economic justice, Tucker resigned to start his own radical review. On 6 August 1881, Tucker's first issue of Liberty appeared, saying:

> This journal will be edited to suit its editor. He hopes what suits him will suit his readers, but if not, it will make no difference. . . . Liberty is published for the very definite purpose of spreading certain ideas, and no claim will be admitted on any pretext of freedom of speech, to waste its limited space in hindering the attainment of that object.

With articles and discussion by Andrews, Spooner, Greene, Heywood, and Ingalls, Liberty continued for 27 years, the longest-lived radical periodical of economic and political nature in the nation's history, and certainly one of the most interesting. Tucker was sure that "political and social structures of American culture could be better dealt with after economic problems were settled. To be effective, Liberty must find its first application in the realm of economics." The legacy handed down by Tucker and Liberty, and by the other individualist anarchists, is an important foundation for understanding decentralization.

5

Henry George: Eliminating Land Monopoly

HENRY GEORGE REPRESENTS another aspect of the decentralist framework. In the last half of the 1800s, he worked to define and eliminate land monopoly. He was born in 1839 in Philadelphia. As a child, he noted the squalor and misery of people in his neighborhood, alongside great wealth and riches. When he was fourteen years old, he left school to work in a store, and two years later he sailed to Australia as a cabin boy. Everywhere the ship docked he saw this contrast between wealth and poverty—in the Mediterranean ports, in Egypt, India, China, and the South Seas.

Henry George wondered whether such conditions existed in the American West, newly opened to white settlement, where people were washing gold from running streams. He went to California to investigate. There, too, he found destitution among beautiful buildings and spacious homes. Poverty *amid* progress was the enigma of modern times. Why was this? He resolved to discover the reasons, and a solution.

As a printer, reporter, and finally editor of West Coast newspapers, Henry George pondered and reported on the disparity of wealth among people. One day, at the edge of San Francisco, he looked for a bit of land on which to build a home for his family. In an open area, with no houses in sight, he asked a man the cost of an acre there. "One thousand dollars," the man answered.

"A thousand dollars for mere space—a vacant acre on which no work had been done," George remonstrated. "I work for a low wage. Why should I give my earnings and my labor to a holder of land who has done no work at all?"

George found in this incident a clue to poverty in the midst of plenty. Workers had to pay nonworkers for space to live. He editorialized on this and waged a vigorous campaign against government grants of land to railways. The railroad companies bought a controlling interest in his newspaper and forced him out. The extraordinary rise in California land values at the completion of the railway confirmed George's contention that poverty was related to, indeed was *caused by*, modern industrial progress.

After years of thinking and writing about the land problem, George published his monumental *Progress and Poverty* in 1879. It was soon to become the most popular and influential book on economics in its time. With pervasive logic, George discussed the nature of land and land values.

George reminded readers that land is uneven in fertility and quality. On good land, a given amount of labor will produce much; on other land, the same labor will produce less; and on still other land, equal labor will produce little or, in some cases, nothing.

When all land is free (as it was for "settlers" who had displaced the native nations), those acquiring land will take the best first. And most people will take more than they need—holding some of it for the future. To hold land idle without using it, George pointed out, is to "withhold" it from others who need it.

George stressed the ethical challenge in this situation. Who, for instance, should have the best, the good, and the poor land? Obviously, those on the best and good land have a natural advantage not shared by those on poor land.

In addition to a difference in fertility value, land acquires a difference in site value or location value. Where people congregate, the value of land rises. The site value of land goes up in proportion to the industry and jobs available near it. In the same way, land-site value increases as public services are made available to the residents on it—for example, as churches, schools, libraries, streets, public services, and utilities are at hand.

George proceeded to show the effects of "rent" on the general wage level. Rent is the difference between the production on the best land in use and the production on the poorest land in use. As population increases push people to less and less productive land, wages will tend to decrease to subsistence level. Then people appeal for charity and government support. Government unwisely seeks to deal with "poverty" by parity, subsidies, pensions, social security, etc. In fact, as George pointed out, the solution to poverty would come only once the land problem was solved.

Since public services largely create the value in land, Henry George proposed a double-pronged solution: Let the local government collect the rent of land to pay for all public services, and remove all taxation from labor products, improvements (buildings, equipment, etc.), sales, and income. To collect land values for community use, and to remove taxes from buildings, would benefit farmers and homeowners, whose values in buildings, equipment, and capital are usually higher than in land values. It would encourage the *use* of land. The use of land would move up to that yielding more than subsistence, and thus raise the general wage level for everybody. Access to land would be without purchase price. Shortly poverty would be eliminated. Liberty and freedom would be advanced.

George presented an alternative both to finance capitalism and to Soviet communism. George differed from both Adam Smith and Karl Marx. Adam Smith would individualize rent, wages, and interest. All three would go into private, individual, and corporate hands—classical capitalism. Karl Marx would socialize rent of land, wages, and interest; all three would go into the hands of the state, i.e., communism.

Henry George would socialize only the rent of land—that is, its fertility and its site value. Use-title to land would remain in the users' hands, as would wages and interest. But wages and interest would result from free action in a free market. Only rent of land would be used by the local community or local government, with all taxes removed from improvements, buildings, and labor products.

George wrote, published, and campaigned valiantly in England, Ireland, Australia, New Zealand, as well as in the United States. Favored by labor, he was candidate for mayor of New York City in 1886. He was defeated, it was reported, by Tammany Hall. He was always the center of controversy. Catholic prelates thought his teachings so contrary to established doctrine that, in 1887, they excommunicated Father Edward McGlynn because of his active support of George's ideas. The Holy Office ruled in 1889 that *Progress and Poverty* was "worthy of condemnation," which meant that bishops could forbid its reading to Catholics in their jurisdiction. Pope Leo XIII wrote "On the Condition of Labor," directed against land reformers. In response, George wrote a long monograph, "The Condition of Labor: An Open Letter To The Pope," so lucid an explanation of the relation of land monopoly to poverty that one Catholic bishop said, "Next to the Bible, Henry George's writings lay claim to my devotion for expressing laws of love and justice." In a rare turnaround, the Church reinstated Father McGlynn in his parish.

Henry George also wrote *Social Problems* (1883), *Protection or Free Trade* (1885), *A Perplexed Philosopher* (1892), and *The Science of Political Economy* (1898). But it was *Progress and Poverty* that placed him in the front ranks of radical thinkers and won many enthusiastic followers, including Leo Tolstoy. It has been used as a university text in logic, so clear is its development from premise to conclusion. John Dewey said,

"One can count on the fingers of two hands those who rank with Plato, and Henry George would be among them." *Progress and Poverty* has been translated into at least thirteen languages. It was estimated that in the quarter-century before 1905, more than two million copies were sold, a larger market than the most popular novels of the time.

In 1897, Henry George was for the second time labor's candidate for mayor of New York. Four days before the election, he died. His funeral in New York City brought such an outpouring of mourners that it is said to have been the largest tribute ever paid a private citizen in the United States. The numbers of people, and the entourage, equaled that of the funeral for President U.S. Grant. On his gravestone were engraved his words:

> Acceptance of the truth I have taught will not come quickly. If that were true, it would have been accepted long ago. But the voice of truth is mighty, and it will come. One day, justice and peace will flood the world, and people will treat land as their common heritage.

The land monopoly is not the only monopoly, but it is the mother of all monopolies. Where George's proposals have been even partially accepted, land sites have become more accessible, business improved, and market exchange freer. Denmark has changed its tax system in this direction under the leadership of the Justice Party, committed to land-value taxation. With it and thousands of cooperatives, Danish citizens have transformed their country into a flourishing, beautiful countryside, supporting a large population in health and comfort. Melbourne, Australia, and sections of New Zealand have flourished under land-value taxation.

Pittsburgh and Scranton, Pennsylvania, have long shown the benefits of a higher tax-rate on land than on improvements, and other cities are moving into this pattern. Southfield, Michigan, near Detroit, became a city of beautiful homes because of reduced taxes on buildings when taxation shifted to site value of land.

Henry George was preeminently a decentralist. Collecting social values of land reduces and would eventually eliminate the monopolies that manipulate profit, wages, and interest. Removing taxes from labor products would insure workers a larger share of the products and wages they produce.

6

The Cooperatives: People Uniting

In 1844, TWENTY-EIGHT struggling weavers in Rochdale, England, established the first cooperative store, distributing earnings to members in proportion to their patronage. From the beginning, this group sold at regular market prices, and returned to each member from the gross profits in proportion to the amount of that person's purchases in the year. This proved to be key to their growth and to returning ownership, control, and direction to people generally in production, marketing, and credit enterprises.

The original capital of the Rochdale weavers was only 28 British pounds, for which each member had saved at twopence a week. A hundred years later, 1944, the Rochdale Society of Equitable Pioneers had 90,000 members and was the largest merchandising business in London. Their method has spread around the world, with outstanding growth in the United States.

Four basic principles undergird Rochdale Corporation: open membership, democratic control, limitation on capital returns, and payment of patronage refunds to member-customers. Any person needing a cooperative's services may become a member (regardless of race, religion, or wealth) by purchasing one or more shares. Each member has one, and only one, vote in all meetings regardless of the number of shares held.

Only a limited interest is paid on capital. The earnings of the business belong to member-customers, and are returned in patronage refunds. If net return above cost is 5%, for instance, each person receives a refund equal to 5% of the amount he spent at the cooperative that year. Thus cooperatives achieve nonprofit operation.

Cooperative enterprises in the United States have a long history. They can vary widely; from the large and prestigious Associated Press to a small farmer's cooperative for burials. There is hardly a human need that a cooperative is not meeting for its members. The following examples are suggestive of the growing cooperative sphere in America in the 1980s.

The credit union is a form of cooperative. Most families at some time—such as when death or illness strikes, or when they want to build a home, or when a young person goes to college—need a source of credit. Banks have been reluctant to make small loans on the personal notes of people with little security—those who need loans the most. By pooling people's savings, a credit union makes it possible for the whole group to meet members' credit needs when they are urgent.

There are tens of thousands of credit unions in the United States and Canada, with, in 1980, 40 million members and more than $60 billion in assets. Most of them are members of Credit Union National Association. Through the association's World Extension Division, credit unions are being set up in developing countries around the world.

All insurance is essentially cooperative activity, pooling savings and sharing risks by a large number of persons. But all insurance companies are not organized along mutual or cooperative lines. Mutual insurance companies develop active control by policyholders; they keep operating costs low, and return to policyholders sizable dividends or premium reductions. Mutual insurance companies put policyholders' money to work in their members' interest. They meet the insurance needs of groups organized around a common interest, such as a farm organization, labor union, community cooperative, or credit union.

Rural farmers' mutual fire insurance companies enable farmers to share fire losses among themselves—with millions of policyholders, billions of dollars of insurance in force, and hundreds of millions of dollars in premium income.

Cooperative health plans have been created mainly to provide a frugal method of paying for medical care that fits the average family income. Members of such plans pay monthly dues to an association that they control, and receive agreed-upon medical services through a staff of doctors and nurses. Patronage refunds are not made, but plans are operated at cost. The pioneer plan was the cooperative hospital at Elk City, Oklahoma. Millions of persons receive health and hospital care on a prepaid basis from group practice/health plans sponsored by communities, cooperatives, labor unions, and employer-employee associations.

Cooperative home ownership of lower and middle-income families has grown rapidly. Well over a hundred thousand people live in cooperatively owned apartment houses in New York City. Many of them are member-owners of projects sponsored by labor unions in the garment industry, dating from 1926. Amalgamated Homes in the Bronx is commonly owned by 1,400 families, and includes a cooperative shopping center and a credit union.

By 1960, 50 of the cooperative stores in the United States had reached the million-dollar mark in annual business. These 50 cooperative supermarkets had more than 150,000 members, and were doing a combined annual business of nearly $100 million. By 1980, there were nearly a thousand consumer goods cooperatives, with a membership of a million families and an annual turnover of $750 million. To be successful, a consumer cooperative must have a volume of business in natural trade areas, large enough to do efficient cooperative wholesaling and some processing. "Co-op"-labeled merchandise has achieved a good reputation for quality and informative labeling.

The Central Cooperative, Inc., of Superior, Wisconsin, since 1917, is one of the four large wholesale cooperatives that deal in consumer commodities and farm supplies on a large scale.

National Cooperatives, Inc., headquartered at Albert Lea, Minnesota, is owned by 18 regional cooperative wholesalers and manufacturers. It makes milking machines and water heaters and procures automobile supplies, hardware, and groceries for its member-groups.

Independent retailers also cooperate. As early as 1887, a group of New York druggists pooled their order for a barrel of Epsom salts. As the chain store began to endanger the independent merchant's position, more and more retailer-owner wholesale houses were established. In 1960, about 100,000 grocers, 80,000 druggists, and thousands of hardware dealers, bakers, furniture dealers, lumberyards, and feed dealers were served by these cooperative wholesalers. Through joint purchasing, they give the independent business one of the advantages of the nationally-integrated chain.

In the late 1960s and 1970s, a surge of small food-buying cooperatives developed. In churches, colleges, neighborhoods—anywhere people came together—they organized for quantity buying of quality food. Revealing their "protest" to the food industry (now the largest in the world), they sometimes call themselves "food conspiracies." One directory of such groups in 1977 listed names and addresses of 2,100 food cooperatives in the United States.

The Connecticut Dairyman's Marketing Association was the earliest agricultural cooperative. In the 1870s, the Grange began cooperative rural stores, and one is still active in Cadmus, Kansas. In the 1890s, fruit growers' marketing cooperatives were organized on the Pacific Coast.

Most of the present cooperative businesses were established during the agricultural depression following World War I. Almost all of the large regional and wholesale manufacturers and farm-supply cooperatives were founded in the 1920s, with the most rapid growth in the depressed 1930s. By 1980, there were 7,500 farm market and supply cooperatives with 6 million members and turnover of $40 billion.

Eighty-nine percent of the U.S. farms had no electricity in 1935. The Rural Electrification Act, passed by Congress that year, provided that any competent borrower willing to furnish service to all farmers of an area who desired it might apply for low-interest, long-term government loans. Nearly all the applications came from cooperatives. From 1935 to 1962, electrified farms increased from 11% to more than 95%. Cooperative electrical distribution rates were reduced and, in some places, cut in half for all rural consumers. Some cooperatives established their own generating plants. In 1980, a thousand rural electric cooperatives distributed electricity to about 9 million members. Their annual payments for electric energy were about $5 billion.

Three national federations serve cooperatives in general. The Cooperative League of the USA, founded in 1916 (and of which Jerry Voorhis, a former congressman from California, was president for many years), includes cooperatives of all types—rural and urban, consumer and producer, supply and service. The League represents American cooperatives in the International Cooperative Alliance in London, which holds a world congress every three years. The American Institute of Cooperation is an educational agency for agricultural cooperatives. It works with land-grant colleges for developing study courses in agricultural cooperation and holds an annual educational meeting on the operation of agricultural cooperatives. The National Council of Farmers' Cooperatives is a conference body composed of many agricultural marketing and supply cooperatives. It performs legal and legislative work in Washington, D.C., and promotes research and expanded markets for agricultural products.

Though the size of some groups jeopardizes decentralist values achieved through smallness, few cooperatives have reached the magnitude of centralized corporations. Cooperators, for the most part, are aware of the pitfalls of great size, and in one-member/one-vote plans, maintain decentralized control. In most cases, local cooperatives practice another decentralist principle, federation (instead of unification), when joining larger or regional groups. This maintains local autonomy in their operations.

Cooperation and cooperatives are decentralist tools, largely in the distribution and marketing aspects of economics. Two important areas by their nature lend themselves to cooperation and await the widespread transfer from private ownership and control to cooperation. These are (1) the use, owning, and transfer of land, and (2) the issuing, valuation, and circulation of money. Cooperative land tenure and cooperative banking are challenges to decentralists and the decentralist revolution that are discussed in later chapters.

7

Ralph Borsodi: Decentralist Supreme

WE HAVE NOTED the American natives, the philosophical anarchists, the Georgists, and the members of consumer and producer cooperatives as some Americans who dissented from authority and struggled for freedom. In our terms they are all decentralists.

So what is a decentralist? Most people will decipher its meaning as the "opposite of a centralist." If a centralist seeks and uses control over others, a decentralist seeks to avoid such control. He or she wants to spread control and decision-making to everyone involved. A man who earned and deserves the title decentralist supreme is Ralph Borsodi. A businessman, economist, philosopher, and author, Borsodi chose to be a man of both ideas and practice. He eminently deserves acclaim as a pluralist, not a monist, and as an integrator, not a specialist.

Ralph Borsodi's concern was good living. In his life and work, one finds a synthesis and integration of the goals and means of other leaders whose thinking contributed to the decentralist framework. He did not always use their contributions exactly as they presented them. Borsodi was a pluralist. He adapted, added to, or improvised upon the plans and principles of his decentralist forebears. He drew from America's early antistatist individualists; he made creative use of Henry George's land-value tax; he applied cooperation to areas as yet largely neglected by America's cooperatives. Everything he did carried a distinct Borsodi stamp. It is crucial to understand his contribution to decentralist thinking and doing, if we intend to make an alternative America.

The son of William and Anna Borsodi, Ralph Borsodi was born in New York City on 20 December 1886, and grew up in lower Manhattan and later in Europe where his mother, suffering terminal tuberculosis, had taken him to visit Hungarian relatives. When she died, he remained until his father remarried four years later. In a somewhat irregular education, he never attended public schools. He had a few years of private schooling, and much informal education in libraries and in his father's home. His father's publishing business was a major source for many books and discussions with authors and writers.

Young Ralph Borsodi devoured the history of the American Revolution and painstakingly followed the debates over the U.S. Constitution in *The Federalist Papers*. Thomas Paine was his hero and companion. In John Locke, Borsodi found a root defense of freedom; in Rousseau's *Emile*, he first came upon "back to the land." Schopenhauer and Nietzsche helped form his belief that "human beings could perfect themselves through a disciplined will."

Borsodi's political and fundamental values came from America's philosopher-economist Henry George and his followers Bolton Hall and Fiske Warren. These men were progressive agrarians, strong in Jeffersonian defense of country life as an alternative to unemployment and other urban discomforts. Modern machines had taken the drudgery out of farm life; AT&T had eliminated distance. Agrarianism and liberty were central in Ralph Borsodi's life-work. Borsodi was active in the Single Tax Party and, as editor of *The Single Taxer*, promoted its central plank of shifting taxation from improvements to land sales.

About 1910, in his mid-twenties, Ralph Borsodi went to Texas to manage several hundred acres of land for his father. What to do with bare land in the wide-open spaces of Texas? Local residents advised Borsodi to hold on to the tract: "People are sure to move from the East to Texas. When they do, your land will go up in price. You might even become a millionaire!"

Borsodi was troubled by this conflict with his principles, this unearned gain in speculative holding of land. To have time to consider his situation, he bought a small-town newspaper, reporting on local happenings and discussing the land problem. Soon he sold his father's acres for a modest figure, leaving the ethics of landholding to a newcomer.

Back in New York City, Borsodi was more than ever aghast at the concrete and brick canyons, with buildings soaring ten or twenty stories into the air. A few blocks away, millions lived in ghettoes. Borsodi saw the connection. Every building, giant skyscraper, or shabby tenement occupied space—a bit of land—the owners of which were growing rich by collecting unearned wealth in rent or selling price of that land. Millions were living on the low wages left after rent was paid. Borsodi determined to do something to change and improve those conditions.

In 1911 Borsodi married Myrtle Mae Simpson, a Kansas farm girl who was in New York City for a career. Finding Manhattan unsuitable to rearing two young sons, the Borsodis moved out of the city in 1919. They went first to Seven Acres, which they remodeled, and then to build, from native rock, in Rockland County, their now famed Dogwoods Homestead, near Suffern, N.Y. They produced all of their food, and most of their shelter and clothing by themselves.

This Ugly Civilization

Borsodi soon began to publish his views in what was to become a large body of important decentralist thinking. In *National Advertising and Prosperity* (1923) Borsodi indicted national-brand advertising for putting false values on many products. In 1926 he exposed top-heavy distribution costs in *This Distribution Age*. In 1928 Macmillan published his over-all critique of modern industrialism, *This Ugly Civilization*, presenting a human alternative, the modern, small-machine-equipped homestead.

"Ours is an ugly civilization," he began. "It is polluted, noisy, hectic, over-consuming natural resources, and murdering time (man's most precious possession) in order to produce more goods. It fails to provide a means of living in which people find enjoyment in, and meaning for, living."

Borsodi presented the modern homestead as an alternative and challenge to industrial factory-workers. He described and showed the implication of Dogwoods Homestead, where he and his family produced from the ground up. They made organic compost by layering vegetable and animal waste, kitchen refuse, and good earth. They tilled the resulting humus, full of living bacteria, into their soil. They planted and harvested green beans, peas, corn, tomatoes, carrots, potatoes, squash, and pumpkins. They cared for a small flock of chickens and their two goats. They pruned old grape vines, berry canes, aging apple and pear trees. They were rewarded with bushels of fruit, although not always of first grade. "It's better to find a worm now and then, than to spray with chemicals," Borsodi said.

He stressed modernity. They used and applied modern electricity and tools: power saws, drills, and sanders; tillers in the garden, canners and an electric mill in the kitchen. A human and decentralist technology eliminated drudgery of home production, Borsodi said, and would thereby lessen the use of factory machines, the chief evil of industrialism.

Factories are of two kinds, observed Borsodi. One kind are essential factories which produce desirable goods which can be made only in factories—wire, pipe, sheet metal, for instance. Then there are nonessential factories which produce either undesirable goods (such as patent medicines or nuclear bombs) or desirable goods, such as food and clothing, which could be better produced at home or in small-scale groups. By Borsodi's measure, more than half of modern factories are nonessential.

This book led to an invitation from Dayton, Ohio, for Borsodi to assist the social agencies in dealing with overwhelming unemployment. Borsodi helped them get people out of the city, to build their own houses, produce their own food, attain a new measure of independence and security on small plots of land. When inadequate financing led to considering borrowing from the federal government, Borsodi explained its risks and dangers. When government money was sought, Borsodi withdrew, returned to Suffern, N.Y., and began the new education he said was essential if ever human values and a decentralist culture were to be achieved.

The School of Living Period: 1936–45

In 1936, Borsodi and friends began an important experiment in adult education which continues today in different forms. The School of Living, as it was called, was dedicated to a new life-style and ethical economic patterns. The school consisted of a Dutch colonial structure at the center of 4 acres, and these acres were surrounded by 16 2-acre family homesteads. Building the homes, developing the homesteads and the community, *was* the education of living. Three new economic patterns were primary.

1. An ethical land-tenure. The Bayard Lane Community, organized as a cooperative-corporation, bought and held title to the 40 acres. Rather than buying its 2 acres outright, each family contracted to use them only for homesteading and pledged themselves to pay a small annual rental to the Bayard Lane Community, of which it was a member, with a vote in policy-making.

2. A cooperative labor policy. The building guilds were associations of workers who planned with a homeowner to build his home for an agreed-on sum. If they finished it at less cost than that sum, the difference was shared between the guild workers and the owner.

3. A cooperative credit system. An Independence Foundation developed a fund, from which to loan to home builders. Effort was made to secure funds at less interest than the market rate charged its homesteader borrowers. This saving was shared between lenders and borrowers.

These activities, plus seminars, workshops, a remarkable library, and a busy productive-gardening schedule, constituted an adult education for a humane culture.

During that time Ralph Borsodi took part in a significant dialogue on small-scale farming with U.S. Department of Agriculture officials, which was published in 1939 as *Agriculture in Modern Life*. In 1940, he wrote his penetrating analysis for economists of exploitative economics in *Prosperity and Security*. In 1943, he predicted *Inflation is Coming*, presenting the family homestead as a personal alternative and commodity-backed currency as a long-range one.

Three problems necessitated the school's sale to a private homesteader in 1945: Mrs. Borsodi's need for care due to a growing malignancy, World War II's shaky economy—reducing the school's income—and a controversy over the community land-tenure.

In 1948, Myrtle Mae Borsodi died, but Ralph Borsodi kept at his crusade. He toured the Far East, and reported it in *Challenge of Asia*, urging that the East improve and continue its family-village culture, rather than aping the industrial West. Later, he established a linotype in the basement of Dogwoods and set, in hot metal, two volumes of *Education and Living*. Completed in 1948, Vol. 1 outlined six centralizations of industrial America; Vol. 2 defined "ranges of normality" and expanded his vision of normal individuals, normal families, normal communities, regions, and world.

Melbourne University

In 1966, Ralph Borsodi and Clare Kittredge were married and moved to Melbourne Homestead Village, established by two former Dayton co-workers, near Melbourne, Florida. Here the Borsodis built a small university for the study of human action. Seminars were held with outstanding panel leaders including Joseph Wood Krutch, naturalist; Paul Tillich, theologian; Philip Wylie, humanist; and Willis Nutting, professor at Notre Dame. With them, seminarians probed The Nature of Man, The Nature of the World, of Truth, of Validating Human Action.

They examined alternative solutions to problems of health, production, distribution, possessions, government, organization, and occupation. This beginning renaissance in education was soon overwhelmed by the influx of the military-industrial complex during the Cape Canaveral buildup.

Concluding that the temper of the United States was not ready for "normal living," the questions it raised, and the education it called for, Borsodi returned to India. In Bombay, at the invitation of Suraum Lotvala, editor of *The Libertarian*, Borsodi wrote A *Pan-Humanist Manifesto*, outlining the essential points for freedom and justice in a humanized world. (It appears at the back of this book as "A Decentralist Manifesto.")

Soon he was guest of Chancellor B. D. Patel of Vidyanagar, a Gandhian university in Ambala. He addressed the faculty on what he called the lack of an integrating factor in modern education. Urged to prepare it, he resumed work on his *Major Problems of Living*. He had barely begun when a controversy developed. Technicians on the faculty who wanted a more "modern approach" objected to an American decentralist on their faculty. The Gandhians defended a do-it-yourself, agrarian-based culture. The technicians won; the Gandhians were deposed; and Ralph Borsodi's writing stopped.

Gandhian friends rallied to develop a social science institute to sponsor Borsodi's work and helped him move to a cooler climate in northern India. There he fell ill. When partially recovered he returned to his wife and to their New England homestead in 1962. For four years he had been well received by the Libertarians and Gandhians in India, "not without honor except in his own country."

The Exeter Period

In Exeter, N.H., Borsodi found and created ample opportunity for his counterrevolution. He resumed regional conferences on Population Control, on Ecumenical Humanism, and on Non-Exploitative Economics. He wrote and published his challenge to general semantics, *Definition of Definition*, calling for a dictionary of precise terms in the social sciences. "Without it," he said, "social scientists cannot communicate, and chaos continues."

During the Exeter period, Borsodi advanced two of his cherished reforms. A younger friend, Robert Swann, came to him for help in opening economic doors for the underprivileged of the southern United States. Together they organized the International Independence Institute to foster and demonstrate ethical access to land, The Community Land Trust, where land is used for a rental fee, rather than purchased outright.

Borsodi set up and operated a year's experiment in the use of a new currency, backed by (and redeemed in) actual staple commodities rather than gold (or nothing, as is now the case with U.S. dollars).

Borsodi completed his *magnum opus*, the definition of seventeen major problems of living and the listing of three alternative solutions to each one, along with bibliographies. With his friends Mary and Maurice Young of Muscatine, Iowa, he flew to Europe to register in the Independence Institute at Luxemburg, and on to India for the third time to arrange publication of *Seventeen Problems of Man and Society*.

In 1973, fifty years after the completion of Dogwoods homestead, Ralph Borsodi and friends celebrated his achievements and some belated recognition in America. The *Bergen County Record* (N.J.) published a full-page account of his experiment with Constants (see Chapter 22). They also issued a supplement to their Sunday edition recording Borsodi's fifty-year effort for decentralization. *Mother Earth News* honored him with two of its Plowboy interviews. He participated in the Dines seminar on money, and *Forbes, Barron's,* and the New York *Daily News* carried stories of his experiment with Constants. At one of several conferences, friends presented him a $1,000 purse and a sheaf of glowing appreciation.

Ralph Borsodi died on 26 October 1977. He was one of the quiet, singularly revolutionary philosophers and achievers of the modern world. For almost a century, Borsodi lived through the complexity of modern times—a booming factory industrialization, the centralization of population in huge cities, the spread of agribusiness—depression years, war years, government support years. Prosperity and affluence had been followed by disillusionment, youth protest, questioning—a yearning for a return by many to more meaningful living. Critics of industrialism are now popular: E. F. Schumacher and Ivan Illich from abroad; Alvin Toffler, Murray Bookchin, and Karl Hess in America. Guided by them and others, many people have begun restructuring their lives and society in decentralist ways. The 1980s portend many important changes.

Ralph Borsodi was a forerunner and prophet of all this, and to him was granted the unusual privilege of seeing his *Ugly Civilization* and *Flight from the City* republished before his death. Many who now turn to Borsodi's life and books, to the School of Living, and to the decentralist movement cherish his legacy for a decentralist world.

Those who know well his lifelong indefatigable energy and unswerving devotion to ethical principles share Dr. Gordon Lameyer's evaluation: "Ralph Borsodi is the Socrates of New Hampshire, the Sam Johnson of the North, the Aristotle of classification in the social sciences, the Free World's answer to Karl Marx, the Gandhi of America, and the best teacher I ever had."

8

The School of Living: Adult Education for Normal Living

EVERYONE IS FAMILIAR with a school of engineering, a school of agriculture, an art school, a trade school, or a beauty school. But Ralph Borsodi was the first to conceive and organize a School of Living to offset the specialization and fragmentation that dominate modern education and living. His was an attempt at wholeness and the fulfillment of human beings by more careful attention to major, universal problems of living. He concluded that if Americans were to recognize the peril in an overindustrialized culture, if they were to maintain a human balance, then a new education of adults was necessary.

Borsodi saw the need for *adult* education. A certain minimum of adult experience in life is necessary if one is to understand the problems of living, and a certain minimum of adult power is necessary if one is to do anything about it. Unfortunately, by the time an individual becomes an adult, he or she has been miseducated for the most part. What was called for, Borsodi emphasized, was "reeducation."

> We begin not with the problems of children but the problems of parents. It is ridiculous to assume that just because men and women have become old enough to support themselves, to marry and perhaps have children, that they are no longer in need of education. In organizing education on this fallacious assumption today, we have in effect turned modern humans over to the tender mercies of advertising men on the one hand, and political demagogues on the other. In making no adequate provision for furnishing adults guidance and leadership in dealing with the problems with which they are for the first time seriously confronted after they become adult, we virtually render worthless whatever we have succeeded in teaching them as children in school and college. If no provision is made in *every community* for the education of

adults by the wisest and most disinterested individuals society produces, the gap in social organization is certain to be filled by a leadership composed of the most aggressive, most selfish, and most short-sighted individuals that society has produced.

A School of Living curriculum would not be an intellectual "department store" with all kinds of courses in every conceivable subject of study. Rather, proponents of the School of Living idea believe that knowledge can be integrated, that it must be integrated, and that organization around basic problems of living leads to integration. Once the major problems are thoroughly understood, then the arts and sciences can be culled for what each has to offer to solving life's real and basic challenges. Without the undergirding of problems, knowledge is a mere collection of "facts and techniques" which may be useless or used in perfunctory or fragmentary ways. Merely "learning how to make money—or earn a living" is not an adequate goal for education; learning how to live understandingly and fully is the true challenge to education.

In the summer of 1934, *The New Republic* published an article by Borsodi on the idea of the School of Living in which he outlined the four major concerns any School of Living would address:

1. the practice of living—the art and science of feeding, clothing, and sheltering the family, and the art and science of health, culture, and play;

2. management—the management of the individual life, of family life, of social life, and of political life;

3. the principle of living—"Past history and current history will be studied as a means of determining future history";

4. philosophy—"not as a discipline, but as an instrument for integrating life and for determining a desirable way of living."

What would be studied and how it would be studied would come out of the problems of everyday living integrating theory and practice.

> If in the course of trying to find the best answer to the question, "Why does bread made with whole wheat flour fail to rise in the same way as that made with white flour?" one is inadvertently betrayed into the study of the whole question of nutrition and the chemistry of foods, it will be a fortunate, but in such a way of living, an inevitable accident. If, in the course of trying to select the best colors in the yarns which are to be woven into the fabric which is to make one's next

winter coat, one is again inadvertently betrayed into the study
of color and discovers the fundamental connection between
the creative crafts and the fine arts, no one, I am sure, will
feel that serious harm has been done to the student.

Significantly, in the first School of Living building at Kakiat Cottage in
Suffern, N.Y., a kitchen was as important as a library and meeting rooms.

The central idea to emerge from the School of Living is not instruction
in country living and in folk arts and handicrafts. Nor is it the
development of a better method of dealing with unemployment, nor the
solution of the housing problem. It is "the scientific validity of
decentralization . . . that the progress and centralization for which
modern industrial man had been taught he should live is based upon a
tragic error."

Borsodi hoped that a School of Living would eventually appear in
every community—in fact, he felt that this was the only hope for
civilization. It would promote individual action, and action in small,
cooperative groups, to improve individual, family, community, regional,
and global life. It would promote healthful living, organic agriculture,
homesteading, "intermediate" technology—in short, normal living in a
decentralized world.

The School of Living

The first School of Living was located near Borsodi's Dogwoods
Homestead. A rented cottage was readied for its new function as a
training center. A meeting room was furnished, books were transferred to
a library, a kitchen was equipped, and a fall garden was planted. Classes,
sessions, and work projects were outlined. And on 3 September 1934
friends and seekers were on hand to celebrate and dedicate the School of
Living in Kakiat Cottage. Forty people gathered in a circle. Ralph
Borsodi spread his arms toward the Ramapos: "I will lift up mine eyes
unto the hills, from whence cometh my help. The rocks, the earth, the
hills! In truth the very source of our life and living. The modern world
needs to learn and relearn this. To such learning, we dedicate a School of
Living."

The father and son planted a small tree from Dogwoods. "Let the tree
be a *symbol* of life and living," said Borsodi.

"Let a tree of life be the *emblem* of the School of Living," said Ralph Borsodi the younger.

"Let the tree remind us that 'Creation dignifies labor, justifies suffering, and gives significance to life,'" Myrtle Mae Borsodi added, quoting the *motto* recently chosen for the School of Living.

Each weekend, attendance increased for informal but serious discussions. Then in 1935, Borsodi and some friends began to talk about beginning a cooperative homesteading association. Forty acres were bought near Dogwoods; sixteen families built charming 2-acre homesteads around the central 4 acres which were reserved for a large School of Living. This building was equipped with everything necessary for self-reliant homesteading and learning—library, kitchen, and various mills, motors, and machines for processing food grown in the nearby gardens.

Here came faculty and students, and the indefatigable Borsodis, to define, discuss, and work at major problems of living. Workshops and seminars were attended by a galaxy of persons, some of whom have become known in decentralist circles: Chauncey Stillman, architect Graham Carey, *Catholic Worker* co-founder Peter Maurin, Georgist W. W. Newcomb, cooperator Morgan Harris, nutritionists Agnes Toms and Paul Keene, pacifists Ralph Templin and Alfred Hassler, professors Richard Dewey and Gordon Lameyer.

At the Bayard Lane School of Living, as it was called, a wide variety of experiments and researches were conducted by a staff of as many as forty persons. Nearly $300,000 was spent under Borsodi's direction before the outbreak of World War II in 1939 made it necessary to end experiments and inquiries. However, significant leaders of modern thought joined in seminars and productive living until 1945. They included Monsignor L. L. Ligutti, now at the Vatican; Benson Y. Landis of the National Council of Churches; T. K. Quinn, author of *I Quit Monster Business;* David Sonquist, director of Circle Pines Co-op Camp; E. C. Riegel, president of the Valun Institute; Ed Robinson of the Have-More Plan; Amon Hennacy, of the *Catholic Worker;* and Mary and S. P. Dodge of the Avon Company of Suffern, N.Y.

After the war much of the school's work was transferred to the Loomis Lane's End Homestead in Brookville, Ohio. A supplementary building was constructed there for the school's library, apprentices, and assistants. Seminars were held all of the time, and visitors constantly dropped by to learn from the school and to add to the excitement of decentralism's way. Larger conferences were organized and held each summer on various college campuses: Oberlin, Earlham, Wittenberg, Antioch.

Ralph Borsodi and I co-edited *The Interpreter*, the school's journal, from 1943 to 1947, and I continued until 1957. During those years, the 8½″ × 11″ publication vigorously presented "decentralist interpretations of current events." Under its masthead were collected many important letters and articles from a diverse group of writers that included Henry A. Wallace, Aldous Huxley, John Gould, Louis Bromfield, Wilhelm Ropke, Willis Nutting, Laurence Labadie, and J. P. Narayan.

In 1958, The School of Living journal changed its format (to *Reader's Digest* size) and took the title *Balanced Living*. Active homesteaders like Rose Smart, Ken Kern, and the Treichlers provided reports on how their life-style was solving major problems of living for them. June Burn, Adelle Davis, and Henry Winthrop added feature articles through 1962.

Robert Anton Wilson (later the author of *Illuminatus*) took over the editorship for two years (1963–64) and changed the journal's title to *A Way Out*. He filled its pages with vigorous articles on anarchism and nonexploitative economics. Herbert Roseman, another short-term editor, produced a collector's issue in October 1967. It was devoted to "Free Land, Free Banking, Free Trade, and Free Men for America."

During those years, the publishing, mailing, and general overseeing of the school's journals remained my responsibility at Lane's End Homestead in Ohio. Many readers became aware that a distinctly decentralist movement was developing in America and responded by saying, "We're excited about *A Way Out*! We're ahead of our time! What we're into is a revolution!"

In those days "revolution" brought visions of Russia and communism— a far cry from our independent, productive life at Lane's End. We were ready for another title that would more clearly describe *our* revolution. Someone suggested *Green Revolution*, and the journal has been published under that name since 1968.

Larry Lack edited *Green Revolution* from 1971 to 1974, with the help of others at one of the first communes, the School of Living's Heathcote Center in Freeland, Maryland. The journal then reflected the seeking and experimenting that were such a part of the times.

The School of Living moved to Deep Run Farm Center near York, Pa., in 1974, and with it went the journal. Rodney Stucki was editor for a few years, and then Rarihokwats (Gerald Gammbill) became the editor in 1979 through the special Spring 1981 issue on Guatemala. The journal is now edited by a committee of four—Mildred Loomis, Hope Taylor, Herbert Goldstein, and Marilyn Dickman. *Green Revolution*, like many of its readers, has had a plucky, innovative, and long life.

In 1965, a property known as The Heathcote Mill, Rt. 1, Freeland, Maryland, was purchased by the School of Living and refurbished to become the headquarters of the school. It was directed by Mrs. Dee Hamilton, Dr. Willis, Lucile Hunting, and a group of resident students headed by Larry Lack. In 1974, George and Ann Shumway of Deep Run Farm, York, Pa., put their 25 acres into a School of Living land trust and arranged the sale of its buildings to the School of Living Deep Run Farm.

The School of Living has been a fellowship in the best sense of that word. All who have expressed an interest have had a say in the workings of the school. Larger matters have been decided on by the nine trustees of the school (three elected each year by members, to serve for three years).

A distinguished and changing Advisory Council is just one indication of the School of Living's influence. Members have included Harry Elmer Barnes, Pitirim A. Sorokin, Paul Goodman, Felix Morley, J. I. Rodale, Adelle Davis, Albert Ellis, Jerry Voorhis, Richard Drinnon, Hazel Henderson, Carter Henderson, Karl Hess, Beatrice Trum Hunter, Kirkpatrick Sale, and Mark Satin. Yet more astounding are the hundreds of men and women who have come to the school and have completely reshaped their pattern of living as a result of what they have learned there. Some of these remarkable people will be discussed more fully in the following chapters.

Manas magazine, itself decentralist in values and emphasis, perhaps best summarized the School of Living in its issue of March 23, 1977. The School of Living is more than a formal lineage dating from the Kakiat Cottage in 1934 to Deep Run Farm today.

> Historians will point out that in the 20th century, the Dark Ages reached bottom, and neither humans nor their planet could stand the way things were going. Social studies may not be needed, considering the changes that will have come about, but there will doubtless be attention to the teaching and examples of Gandhi and Vinoba Bhave and some study of the works of pioneers like Arthur Morgan and Ralph Borsodi.
>
> Borsodi, for example, called for radical change in 1928 with his book, *This Ugly Civilization,* and a year or so later, he published an account of the direction his own life was taking in *Flight from the City.* He described his homestead in Suffern, N.Y., where he founded the School of Living in 1936.
>
> Awareness of the need for schools of living has grown apace. Today, whether or not their inspiration is traceable to

the pioneering of Borsodi and his colleague Mildred Loomis, there are many similar efforts under way, some of them actual schools on a piece of land somewhere, some centers located in cities where inventive individuals are discovering and teaching ways to transform sterile urban areas into vital neighborhood communities.

Some of the new magazines amount to "schools of living," with contents devoted to practical means of creating new ways of self-support and living on the land. For example, *Rain* of December 1976 tells about a designer and manufacturer whose ingenious and comfortable canvas furniture wins prizes and who says, "I feel a void when the basis for my contact with people is money."

More and more people are refusing to found their lives on the cash nexus. Every person who attempts this freedom is conducting a school for living in his various relationships.

9

The Green Revolution
Christened

IN 1940, A GROWING group of persons concerned with the quality of
life, rather than with the overriding desire for things, were becoming
interested in decentralization. In the School of Living circle, more and
more persons found their lives becoming integrated. In homesteading,
they could be honest, practice social justice, experience personal growth,
and live in harmony with nature. This trend received a name in a
dramatic meeting at the School of Living in 1940.

In that year, School of Living forums were well received by progressives
and radicals in New York City. Persons came as leaders and students from
various groups. World War II had begun, and serious people probed
deeply. A particularly thoughtful group at the education seminar in
January 1940 included Stringfellow Barr, president of St. John's College
of Annapolis; Morgan Harris, educational director of a major cooperative
in New York City; William W. Newcomb, Georgist editor; Graham
Carey, noted sculptor; Peter Maurin from the *Catholic Worker*; plus
several teachers, homesteaders, and the School of Living staff.

Seminar members outlined their primary concerns and solutions for
social ills. Graham Carey mentioned his debt to English distributists
Hilaire Belloc and Eric Gill and showed how art and responsibility are
joined—both result from human work. A man tending a machine that
makes boxes uses very little of his capacities. A craftsman carving a
wooden bowl, on the other hand, uses his whole self—mind, body, will,
and feeling. He is therefore fully responsible for the object he makes.
According to Graham Carey, then, a reform in work is the principal need
of modern industrialism.

"No. The land problem is the first needing solution," maintained Bill
Newcomb. He outlined the thesis of Henry George and showed its
relation to the on-to-the-land homesteaders. "Homesteaders are blocked
by the high price of land. And nations go to war for profit in land and

minerals. Land monopoly causes depressions and unemployment. Family security and world peace depend on ready access to land."

"I maintain that cooperation is the first need for a better world," Morgan Harris offered. "Competition is our ruination; cooperation is an alternative." He showed how consumer cooperative groups eliminated middlemen.

Dr. Barr described the Great Books Program at St. John's College as a way to define and probe universal problems and develop motivation and skill in solving them.

Mrs. Borsodi said, "I think the world's first need is good communication to help us reach agreement easily. That takes psychological insight and emotional maturing."

"And much adult immaturity comes from faulty child training," put in a teacher. "In my view nothing outweighs the loving, free relationships between adults and children. Children must have freedom to experiment and grow at their own pace and initiative."

Ralph Borsodi spoke. "You have all touched immensely important problems. You have demonstrated the complexity of education for living. Our need is for agreement on what constitutes universal *major* problems of living—the underlying and important ones—and of implementing human solutions for them. The School of Living attempts this. We see Graham Carey dealing with occupation. Bill Newcomb focuses on the possessional problem—who shall own land, goods, and other wealth. Morgan Harris sees the importance of how to organize enterprises. Of course, communication, child-parent relations, and Great Books are important. Let's develop an education that includes and integrates all."

We sat by the fire, late into the night, seeking common ground.

In the morning, Bill Newcomb summarized: "Each of us has a special ax to grind, a special reform to sponsor for that better world. Our professions and our work represent what is most important to us. Here at the School of Living, we've had a new concept of a good life and an education for a good society. We've seen a larger whole. Each of our specialties is necessary, but not adequate alone."

"The School of Living's job is synthesis—integration," Bill continued. "The School should *federate*—not actually *unite* us. That confederation would be a new movement. It needs a name. What should it be?"

Suggestions came. "The School of Living Movement." "Decentralization." "The New Age."

A sturdy peasantlike friend stood up. "I'm Peter Maurin of the *Catholic Worker*, just over from France," he said. "This morning the paper says

Nazi planes are bombing my country. Troops are pouring across the border. Refugees are stranded along the highways, in the area of my home, my friends, and my family." He stopped and we waited.

"My people love life and the land. In every country, there are those who do. The only hope I see for the world is in the spirit and works like School of Living. In France, we call it The Green Revolution." For a while, no one spoke.

"Good," said one. "I agree," another said. "Me too," from a third. Several nodded. Consensus was reached, and at lunch Morgan Harris raised his glass of carrot juice, proposing, "Long life to the Green Revolution!"

The term found acceptance. Some used it in *Free America*, in *The Christian Century*, the *Catholic Worker*, and of course, in School of Living's *Interpreter*. From that beginning in 1940, The Green Revolution was our term for the decentralized, organic culture we worked for. In 1963, it became the official title of the School of Living monthly, *The Green Revolution*.

Gradually the term Green Revolution spread. We reported on family homesteads, organic agriculture, activities in small communities. We discussed freeing the land of price and speculation, cooperative credit, a stable exchange medium, replacing government with voluntary action.

The Green Revolution Misappropriated

The School of Living had used the term Green Revolution for nearly thirty years. We were glad for the response, and thrilled at the meaning added to it by intelligent homesteaders, editors, and journalists. We were pleased with the spread of the concepts and practices of an organic green revolution. Pleased—but not entirely satisfied. Who can be satisfied with slow-motion of what is felt to be vital for human welfare as a decentralist revolution amid wholesale centralization? We continued working for, and welcoming, any evidence of change in the decentralist direction.

In the spring of 1968, our treasured term leaped out from headlines in the daily paper: "Green Revolution to Feed Starving Millions." Biologist Norman Borlaug of Indiana University was in Mexico, experimenting with improved yields of wheat. He had developed wheat with yields ten times greater than ordinary wheat. This, said the newspaper account, was a "green revolution."

"Good!" I thought, and read on. Borlaug and the persons heading this "green revolution" were hardly decentralists. The new wheat and rice would be grown in thousand-acre fields; they required lots of water from irrigation. With these new grains were exported huge harvesting machines, tons of chemical fertilizers and sprays to fend off fungi and insects. *This* was a "green revolution"?

"Plagiarism, travesty, misuse of our thirty-year-old term," I protested. Such practices would not really help. They were what *our* green revolution had rejected three decades ago!"

Not more than a year later, a different tone appeared in public reports of this "new" green revolution. In April 1969, scientist C. R. Wharton titled his article in *Foreign Affairs*, "Is the Green Revolution Cornucopia or Pandora's Box?"

"The green revolution," he said, "is straining investment capital to buy large tracts of land needed for the new program and its big machines. Native skill was not available to handle the machines, nor were there mechanics for repairing their breakdowns. Consequently, harvesters are left to rust in the fields."

And then in August 1974, I noted a color-jumbled headline: "Green Revolution Future is Black." This article reported that Borlaug and *his* green revolution advocates had made a mistake. Monocultured, chemically fertilized, and sprayed grains were subject to disease.

"The spread of disease by this large-scale mono-crop agriculture could bring about serious worldwide starvation. A whole season's production could be wiped out. The 'green revolution' was a mistake!" Who released this report? None other than the United States Department of Agriculture.

Decentralists and organic farmers could nod our heads. As Ralph Borsodi wrote to me,

> The past thirty years have laid a foundation for rethinking our country's wealth and power, and its agriculture along with it. There's ample proof now that only one revolution is green— the one that enriches the soil, that gives people both security and freedom, the one that enhances, not threatens, life. I believe we are on the verge of a real, green, postindustrial and decentralist revolution.

Many events and activities in addition to the ones chronicled in this book confirm that a valid movement was christened in 1940. Its name has withstood abuse. As we have moved into the 1980s, the cheer rings firmer and stronger, "Long live the Green Revolution!"

10

Rodales at the School of Living

WHEN I ASSISTED at the Suffern, N.Y., School of Living, we never knew what special event each day might bring. One 1940 spring morning, I answered a knock to greet two people, relatively unknown then but who later influenced American decentralism more than almost anyone else in this century.

"I'm J. I. Rodale from Emmaus, Pennsylvania," the man said, "and this is my son Robert. I have an appointment with Mr. Borsodi."

While the two men talked, Robert helped Reece and Betty May feed their rabbits and chickens. At the time, Rodale was editor of the *Journal of Lexicography*. But his growing concerns in 1940 were agriculture and America's declining health. About these, he and Borsodi exchanged views. Borsodi showed him the library, with books shelved under major problems of living. Rodale spent several hours with the health problem group and at lunch exclaimed, "For me, your library is a gold mine! Scores of books which I need. That one small book by Dr. G. T. Wrench, *Wheel of Health*—fantastic! All about the remarkable people in the Himalayas, the Hunzas! Sturdy at more than a hundred years of age, mostly because of their natural food grown in such good soil."

Delighted, Borsodi nodded and joined in, "On a diet of apricots, wheat, and goat milk, especially from their specially fertile soil. Of course, the exercise in producing that food helps give the Hunzas their remarkable record!"

There was other table talk. "These muffins, Mrs. Borsodi, are excellent," Rodale said.

"Made from our own flour ground in our electric kitchen mill, which we'll show you soon."

"You eat from your own supplies, entirely?" he asked.

"Almost," Mrs. Borsodi went on. "The beans are from our garden, frozen and stored over winter. The carrots and apples in the salad are from our root cellars. And the ice cream is from Nellie's milk, with our own honey added."

After lunch we toured the homestead, the gardens, the compost heaps, and stopped in the barn to pat Nellie and her new calf. Then Rodale went back to the library, to take notes.

"These are the things Americans need to know" J. I. Rodale said in 1940. "These would stem degeneration and disease. With them Americans could build health and stamina. I want to help them do it. I must study, experiment, and publish what I learn."

His search took him far into the chemistry of food and soil; into questioning the use of chemicalized commercial fertilizers. He learned of the Soil Association in England, and of the biodynamic agriculture of Ehrenfried Pfeiffer. He made plans for new publications.

In 1948, J. I. Rodale began a radical new approach to health in a monthly journal, *Prevention*. To prevent, rather than cure, disease cut across accepted and deep-rooted views of medicine and health. The response was good. The skill, wisdom, and persistence of the Rodales and a growing staff extended subscriptions and impact rapidly.

Five years later (1953), Rodale began publishing *Organic Gardening* as a companion monthly to elaborate on the theory and practice of organic gardening. Very early, he published Ralph Borsodi's research, including the School of Living's experiment discovering the lower cost of preparing organic compost, as against purchasing chemicalized fertilizers. People's interest in, and their questions about, how to garden organically, what to do and where, continued.

As the years went by, the Rodales expanded their coverage to many aspects of homesteading: building, repairs, equipment, philosophy, reports, book reviews, questions, and answers. A typical issue might have articles on Food Storage, Stocking up for Winter, Canning it Right, Building a Low-Cost Dryer, Using a Home Freezer. They even included social and cultural implications of decentralization. The Rodale journals are an ongoing part of the decentralist revolution in America. They led (and lead) the way to a flow of books and magazines that practically saturate America in the 1980s.

11

A Decentralist Response to Global Crisis

In 1940, THE Borsodis relinquished active direction of the School of Living program. At the same time, World War II upset the general economy, and financial support for the school dropped off. While a new staff administered the school, the Borsodis retired to Dogwoods to write and travel.

In 1941, Ralph and Lila Templin and Paul and Betty Keene were student-apprentices at the school. Both men had been Methodist missionaries in India and assisted Gandhian forces in their crusade for independence from Britain. For this, the Methodist Board dismissed them from their posts. Returned to their homeland, they decided that the School of Living was "the closest thing to Gandhi in America." They visited, stayed on, and were glad to take over supervision and direction of the school while the Borsodis rested and traveled.

The Templins and Keenes began at once a full program of self-sufficiency: living frugally, planting and producing, and inviting students to share the program at a small fee. They improved the school's relations with the community homesteaders and extended cooperative activities during the troubled World War II years.

Convinced pacifists, the Templins saw decentralization as a nonviolent social pattern, consistent with their values. They presented decentralization to the peace movement. They organized a correspondence course of School of Living tenets and community building. It was studied by men in civilian public service camps, and in prison for conscientious objection to war. A crescendo was reached at the 1944 conference of the Fellowship of Reconciliation at Lakeside, Ohio, when Paul Keene emphasized self-education and self-development via communities and Schools of Living as nonviolent ways to transform people and society. Among those affected, who became future decentralist leaders, were Robert Swann, co-founder of the Community for Non-Violent Action, editor George Yamada, and Sonnewald Homesteader H. R. Lefever.

Responding as they did to the world crisis, the Templins encouraged Ralph Borsodi to write and publish on the global implications of decentralism. And so he turned from the problems of family and community organization to problems of world reconstruction. He saw that certain principles applied at all three levels, but structuring global organization deserved special and careful rethinking in the midst of such a terrible war.

Borsodi was aware of plans for a League of United Nations, or a World Federation of Nations. But he was sure that "nation" was an outmoded concept—an immoral, coercive institution. Nations should relinquish their sovereignty. That was Borsodi's unique organizational proposal! Not a confederation of nations—*eliminate* nations. Let families and communities reclaim their basic functions; and distribute necessary administrative or "policing" functions to decentralized and regional groups.

The Elements of World Peace

In place of the nation-state Borsodi suggested the creation of three entities. He discussed these in a School of Living pamphlet, *A Plan for World Peace by Way of a World Patrol.*

The first global entity would be a world authority. It was clear to him that ores, minerals, oils, and fuels are the gifts of nature to *all* humankind. From them, *all* people—not individuals, rulers, or corporations—should benefit. Rather than treat such mineral resources as commodities for profit and sale, Borsodi advocated a basic principle of Henry George's for global collection of their economic rent. The authority would be restricted to one function—it is not a world government with overall legislative, administrative, and judicial powers. A world authority would only collect the land-site value, or economic rent, of mineral, fuel, and oil resources, and would allocate that to a world patrol force.

A world patrol force would be different from a military force, Borsodi said. A world patrol force would consist of voluntary members, selected by civil service examination, from all parts of the world. It would have one duty—to patrol the land and seas to locate and inactivate any armament installations. It would encircle such armament facility—

factory, ship, or troops—and prevent movement into or out of such facility. Financial support of a world patrol force would be the economic rent-fund of the world authority.

Violators would be reported to a world court empowered to deliver judgment against such individual, corporate, or government violators.

Thus world peace would be obtained and insured, by effectively denying the profit incentive in dealing with world minerals, through channeling the economic-rent of minerals, fuels, and oils to the benefit of mankind, a new type of world authority, and world patrol. These would correct three fatal flaws in current world organization for peace, Borsodi said. It would eliminate nations; it would remove the primary cause for world conflict—the struggle for mineral and oil deposits; and it would give the world authority an arm—the world patrol force—sufficiently coercive, but not violent, to prevent the making and use of armaments. Without armaments, there could be no war.

12

Agnes Toms and Whole Food

OF THE SEVERAL facets of a decentralist revolution, one of the first to capture and hold people's interest was a change in nutrition and diet. Good eating is not only a prime need for survival, but it is also a gastronomic pleasure. It's a simple dictum that says, "You are what you eat." The further one gets into the miracle of soil becoming food, becoming flesh, blood, and bones, the more fascinating the study becomes. It is fortunate that this is so, for the difficult process of changing habits—including food habits—needs all possible support.

By 1940, most Americans had fallen into a host of personal and social errors. In his faith in big cities, big industry, and big government, the average American had become an unthinking and helpless victim of packaged, devitalized foods. Big commercial agriculture, with its depleted soil, chemicalized fertilizers and sprays, and wrong tilling had replaced a more traditional and healthy way of raising and making food. Junk and snack foods sometimes labeled "The Terrible Ten," were everywhere: white bread, doughnuts, coffee, sugar, packaged sweetened cereals, carbonated sugar drinks, potato chips, hot dogs, sweetened baby foods, and "smoked" meats.

The School of Living called for a halt to this modern and tragic trend. It set a standard with its program of composted soil, organic gardening, home preparation and eating of natural whole foods, home grinding of grain, home-baked bread, careful storing and preservation of fruits and vegetables. To most of the School's students, this was new and challenging.

Eight books in the school's library were especially important in advancing a holistic approach to health. Each book and its author contributed to the history of decentralization, and they are still valid reading today. They give something of a historical perspective on the food-reform movement.

Eight Relevant Challenges to Conventional Nutrition

First in time and importance is a small book, *Bread*, by Sylvester Graham, published in 1837. Simply and directly he explained why food is best in its natural state:

> If people were to subsist wholly on substances in their natural state, or without any artificial preparation by cooking, then they would be obliged to use teeth freely in masticating, and in so doing, keep teeth in sound health. At the same time, they would thoroughly mix food with saliva, and thus prepare it for swallowing and for action for the stomach. People would swallow food slowly as the welfare of the stomach and the whole system requires they should.

Further, Graham pointed to deterioration in food caused by improper tillage of the soil

> I have no doubt it is true that the flour and wheat raised on a soil cultivated with a recently-applied crude, stable manure may readily be distinguished by its odor from the flour of wheat raised on a new and un-depraved soil, or from wheat raised on a soil dressed with *properly digested* manure.
>
> If similar results of improper tillage can become sources of serious evil to the human family, through their effects on the flesh of animals which man devours, and on the milk and butter which he consumes, surely the immediate effect of vegetable matter on the same human system must be considerable.

He enumerated the constituents of wheat—starch, sugar gluten, wheat germ, bran (the mucilage of wheat bran is soothing to the stomach and intestines)—and showed how to bake good bread with coarse, whole-grain flour.

The Lee Foundation for Nutritional Research (Milwaukee, Wisconsin), which has done so much to advance the literature of good food, reprinted this significant treatise on bread in the 1950s.

A second challenge came early in the 20th century when it was proven that most body illness did not come from germs and bacteria, but was a systemic, body condition of malfunctioning cells, glands, and organs. *Toxemia Explained* by Dr. John Tilden explained that poisons and toxins in the body resulted from faulty or deficient nutrition, or from overeating, or from the wrong combination of foods.

A third book bringing controversy was the report on the Hunzas, that remarkable people in northern India, many of whom live to 100 and even 120 years of age with such sturdy health that their old men carry burdens over crags and peaks for missionaries and explorers. G. T. Wrench, an English medical official in India, was one of the first to bring the Hunza story to the West. He addressed the American Medical Association in 1921, giving his significant findings from Hunza, with little or no response. It was only when his book, *The Wheel of Health*, was published that the information began to affect the nutrition movement. A few copies were circulated by the School of Living. J. I. Rodale saw it there, and the book was later publicized and distributed by Rodale Press.

Since that time those who have gone to Hunza and later written books on it include J. I. Rodale (*Healthy Hunzas*), Allen Banik (*Hunza Land*), Renee Taylor (*Hunza: Himalaya Shangri La*), and Art Linkletter.

There were also writers who stressed the relation of humus-laden soil to well-balanced, healthy plants and the healthy animals who ate the plants. F. H. King in 1902 developed the thesis in his book titled *Soil*. He described Chinese agriculture in 1935 in *Farmers for Forty Centuries*.

Sir Albert Howard of England and Weston Price, a Cleveland dentist, detailed how and why impoverished soil encourages plant, animal, and human disease. Soil depleted of organic humus loses its trace minerals, resulting in imperfect synthesizing of protein in the green leaf. Gradually, nature's protection in the living cell is lost. Only by obeying nature's law of return—the return of all vegetable, animal, and human wastes to the soil—will such conditions be reversed. High-nitrogen, sulfurized, chemical fertilizers must be avoided. Of the hundreds of books later written on the theory and experiments of compost and its effect on soil and health, all are in some way a repetition or elaboration of Sir Albert Howard's work in India, reported in *The Agricultural Testament*, and quickly followed by his *Soil and Health*.

Weston Price's *Nutrition and Physical Degeneration* was the result of his world tour of countries where people lived on native, well-cared-for soil. Hundreds of photographs in his 525-page book show that people living on native food from virgin soil had broad dental arches and superb health. That was true whether their diet consisted of goat milk and cheese in Switzerland, grains in Africa, rice in India, or fruit in the South Sea Islands. Members of the same peoples who had turned from native diet to white sugar, white flour, and tinned meats of the West had rampant tooth decay and narrowing dental arches.

Thus did eight revolutionary books challenge the traditional 19th-century view of health and healing.

The valiant authors of these books stood in the path of industrialism's juggernaut. Where their messages were heeded, the damage of agribusiness has been moderated. In spite of these books, however, the modern world has been swept into an energy-and-resources crisis of worldwide proportions. (Probably the most effective alert to the fragility of the earth and the emergency of sheer survival was Rachel Carson's *Silent Spring*, [1962]. Revolutionaries of the 1960s found ammunition in her documented proof of harm from chemical fertilizers and overpopulation. Unless such trends were reversed, she said, a spring would come when no more birds would sing.)

In these seminal books, the basis for a revolution in food, nutrition, and agriculture was available in the School of Living library in the early 1940s. There has been much written on health and nutrition since then, and it has very often been an extension, elaboration, and confirmation of the ideas and practices in those eight books.

An Early Food Pioneer

Agnes Toms was one of the early pioneers in food reform. All of her formal training had been in the orthodox ideas and methods of teaching nutrition. She was a graduate of the University of Southern California and had a master's degree in home economics from Columbia University in New York City. She had taught conventional home economics in California high schools for ten years. But a three-week seminar with Ralph Borsodi opened her eyes. Day after day, Borsodi's lectures, along with reading in the school's library, changed her concept of health from the older medical position to the new world of natural healing via food, nutrition, and agriculture.

She was convinced of the wisdom and importance of the school's work and in 1940 she gladly took over management of its food program under the helpful guidance of the Borsodis.

For breakfast for from four to twenty students, Agnes Toms ground grains—wheat, oats, rye, buckwheat, barley—in the electric kitchen mill. A favorite cereal was whole-wheat kernels from a nearby farm, soaked overnight and steamed for an hour the next day. With honey from the school's bees and cream from the cow, the cereals were delicious and nutritious.

Apples were always available. Homestead fruits were canned or frozen—chiefly blueberries, in great supply. Many fruits were dried in a dryer invented by Ralph Borsodi. Fertile eggs from chickens who scratched in the ground and ate live bugs, worms, and bacteria added to the nutrition. Mrs. Borsodi and Agnes Toms made or supervised making all the cottage cheese, butter, yogurt, and ice cream eaten there. Ham, bacon, and sausage were from the school's animals. Time-saving electrical equipment assisted: range, chopper, blender, grinder, refrigerator, freezer, and the cherished flour mill.

People said they had never tasted anything so good as the bread made each day from freshly ground flour. Honey, molasses, and freshly ground peanut butter were so good they had trouble keeping them on hand. For lunch, fruit, melons, and berries—fresh in summer, frozen in winter—accompanied fresh bread, a hot vegetable soup, and a green salad. They followed Borsodi's recommendation to increase vegetables and decrease meat consumption.

The evening meal was a gala affair, with people enjoying vegetables, a raw fruit salad, with chicken, duck, turkey, fish, or a favorite bean-cheese casserole. Everyone helped prepare the popular biscuits, muffins, and breads of whole-grain flour. Desserts were ice cream, fruit cobblers, or shortcakes of whole flour. People often lingered at the fireplace with fresh fruit or berries, cheese, and coffee. Snacks at the School of Living in the mid-1940s were home-grown sunflower seeds, peanuts in the shell, popcorn, and apples, or raisins and dates bought in bulk from organic farms in California.

Robert and Agnes Toms returned to California in the late 1940s, ever grateful for Borsodi's leadership and the School of Living library in those beginning years of the natural foods movement. Agnes again taught foods and nutrition, but this no longer included the use of refined, processed foods. She could not recommend pasteurized milk, or work with foods grown on chemically treated soil or sprayed with poisons. She located sources of natural foods.

But since there were no textbooks from the organic, natural point of view, she wrote her *Delicious and Nutritious*, the first natural foods cookbook ever published. From long use in the Monrovia, California, public schools, it spread widely. Her students had projects to spread the word, such as one group that baked and distributed whole-grain bread at the Los Angeles County Fair.

Patterned after Dr. F. M. Pottenger's experiment with cats, one of Agnes Toms's high school classes fed groups of mice different diets. One group had whole grains, cheese, and fats; another had packaged, commercial cereals, pasteurized milk, and processed cheese. Students were amazed at the results. The whole-foods mice had large well-formed bodies, sleek hair, lively habits, and litters of several babies. Mice on packaged foods were small and scrawny, with body sores. They were alternately quarrelsome or listless, with small or no litters.

Newspapers began reporting Agnes Toms's exhibits and teaching methods. Soon, a large file bulged with clippings about "Natural Foods Being Taught in Public Classroom."

In 1948, she joined the American Academy of Applied Nutrition, a group of doctors, dentists, and other professionals seeking the prevention of disease. They were impressed by the books that had influenced her at the School of Living, particularly those of Weston Price, Sir Albert Howard, and F. M. Pottenger. She reviewed books, lectured, and demonstrated in the Academy's adult study groups.

Since 1960, Agnes Toms has provided columns for *Modern Nutrition,* monthly of the American Nutrition Society; *Natural Foods,* of the Natural Food Associates; and *Let's Live.* In 1974, her second popular book was published, *Natural Food Meals and Menus for All Seasons.* Through Agnes Toms, Borsodi had a basic and notable effect on America's food.

Later Food and Nutrition Literature

Since the 1930s, authors and books on the nutritional approach to health began a continuing flood. Heading the list in sales and influence is Adelle Davis's popular trio: *Let's Eat Right, Let's Cook It Right,* and *Let's Have Healthy Children.* *Reader's Digest* featured her. Use of her "power foods" (wheat germ, yogurt, brewer's yeast) has become a badge for acceptance into the avant garde where Adelle's name is a household word.

Equally popular was Cathryn Elwood, who in *Feel Like a Million* dispensed scientific nutrition in a cheery lively manner. Both Cathryn and Adelle grew up on commercial foods. Both were sickly and under par until they learned good nutrition. Both had college degrees in nutritional research. When they began practicing what they preached, both achieved youthful vigor, each living until nearly eighty years of age.

Another writer is Beatrice Trum Hunter, whose titles include *Natural Foods, Gardening Without Poisons,* and *Consumer Beware!*

Dr. Royal Lee of the Lee Foundation for Nutritional Research has reprinted millions of informative pamphlets. The School of Living's *Interpreter* quoted from and featured him as early as 1950.

Scores of groups have formed to educate on specific aspects of the developing controversy between natural and artificial foods. The Natural Food Associates of Atlanta, Texas, of which Dr. Joe Nichols was president for 25 years, emphasizes whole food from fertile soil. Natural Food Associates was formed in 1951 through the efforts of several young farmers, including Alden Stahr of Layton, N.J., and Robert Rowe of Illinois. They published two volumes of *Normal Agriculture,* later to be titled *Natural Living.* Articles about Lane's End Homestead, Ralph Borsodi, and Paul Keene appeared in their October 1953 issue. Their membership journal, films, and conferences influence hundreds of thousands of people. In 1975, they began developing an 800-acre demonstration farm near their headquarters.

The National Health Federation stresses freedom of choice in health matters. It constantly lobbies against laws that restrict individuals in their learning about health, or in choosing their own method of healing, including nontraditional ones. Headed by Oscar Crecelius in California and Clinton Miller in Washington, D.C., it champions freedom from medical monopoly. It also questions the right of any governmental authority to add fluorides to public water, and it opposes attempts to classify vitamins as drugs or to impose restrictions on the sale of food supplements.

Dr. Herbert Shelton heads the Natural Hygienists (San Antonio, Texas). Hygienists hold that good health results only from living by six natural laws: eating natural foods, drinking pure water, breathing pure air, having adequate physical exercise and satisfying sex, thinking constructively, and feeling positively. Hygienists are developing a 1,600-acre homesteading community near their headquarters.

Jay Dinshah of Malaga, N.J., helps stage a world conference of vegetarians each summer. In 1975, more than a hundred leaders shared with 2,000 delegates from all parts of the globe in a wide spectrum of health education. In 1977, their world congress was in New Delhi, India.

Health Foods—A New Business

Now that health foods are in demand, they are available both on supermarket shelves and in special stores. Directories of bona fide health stores list thousands in all parts of the country. Production, distribution, and sale of health foods claim the attention of business experts. Beginning in the 1930s with Deaf Smith County (Texas) wheat, health food firms now include busy Shiloh Farms in Oklahoma and Pennsylvania and Erewhon Distributors in Boston. Nutrition firms tell millions of homemakers about natural foods in *Family Circle* and *Woman's Day*. Bob Hoffman, York, Pa., businessman and physical therapist, has seen his special protein foods find national acceptance through free distribution of an informative journal, *World Health and Ecology News*. Spontaneous food buying cooperatives, sometimes called food "conspiracies," number in the thousands.

Members of the American public have changed their attitudes about nutrition a lot since the 1930s. Not all have been persuaded, however. Housewives still wheel enormous carts of devitalized, packaged foods from supermarkets. But Agnes Toms and many others are thankful for the books commented on at the beginning of this chapter—and for the many other books like them. The continuing swing to natural foods, natural healing, and natural agriculture is part of the revolution for decentralization.

13

Walnut Acres: Choosing to Stay Small

THE LIVES OF Paul and Betty Keene were changed at the School of Living. In 1940, after a teaching stint in India, the Keenes spent a summer on the farm of a friend in the Catskill Mountains. They loved the soil and loved working in it. In nearby Suffern, N.Y., they found the School of Living with "intellectuals doing things with their hands." They read the home-production *How to Economize* bulletins and were fascinated by the savings they made following them.

That fall, teaching math and physics at Drew University "didn't seem right." Paul's work on his doctoral thesis was distracted by visions of fertile fields, barns and animals, and tender growing things. Realizing they were marching to a different drummer, the Keenes knew they were destined for the country. In the spring of 1941, they became co-directors of the School of Living with the Templins.

"Our two years there," they say, "were rich and formative beyond all asking. The school's students and teachers were pioneering into the future. At its heart was the library with incredible ideas, many of whose time had come. And there to challenge, interpret, direct, and expand stood the Borsodis—original thinkers, indefatigable doers, born teachers." For the Keenes, the homestead had come alive. They caught a glimpse of the oneness and wholeness of life.

Close by, in Spring Valley, N.Y., was Three-Fold Farm, its program based on the teachings of Rudolf Steiner in Germany. Fred and Alice Heckel had studied biodynamic farming there, and helped establish the methods in the School of Living program—companion planting, and compost heaps with special starter made from chamomile, stinging nettle, and other herbs, along with hormones from animal entrails.

The Keenes' work at the School of Living inspired them to make their complete living from organic farming. After two years at Kimberton Farm's Steiner School, they felt ready to go on their own. During their first year on rented land, they suffered the tragic loss of all their crops in July hail storms, which washed much of their soil into the Delaware River. They borrowed $5,000 to buy a hundred acres of rolling land in central Pennsylvania, with house, barn, and sheds. In March 1946, Paul, Betty, their two children, Betty's father, a team of horses, a dog, ancient bits of furniture, and an old car moved to their own farm, Walnut Acres.

Early German settlers had looked for black walnut trees as indicators of the limestone soil they sought. In Penns Creek, Pennsylvania, their new farm was full of them, some of which stood, no doubt, when William Penn lay claim to all land thereabouts.

No mother ever looked more fondly on her newborn than Paul and Betty viewed Walnut Acres as they rattled proudly up the winding lane by the stream. Glory was everywhere. The tin roofs were rusted through in spots? Set buckets under the drips until there is time to patch the holes. Buildings haven't been painted in twenty years and windows falling out? Ah, but the wood is sound—just paste papers over the holes for now. No plumbing, no bathroom, no telephone, no furnace—they must heat with wood? But isn't it great to pioneer? They must live and pay off the mortgage with one team of horses, an old plow and harrow? Well, they had lived on nothing before. Now they had a house and barns and a hundred acres!

The years went by. Soon there were three children and two teams of horses. Then the horses left and a tractor came. And there were cows, sheep, chickens, ducks, geese, bees, rabbits, cats, and dogs. How soon all grew together into one family, each knowing and accepting the other, albeit sometimes grudgingly.

Life returned to their soil. They built terraces, grassed waterways and contour-strips to control water runoff. They planted clover and alfalfa everywhere and allowed heavy sods to grow. They chopped grasses and legumes back into the soil instead of making hay with all of them; they left all the straw on the ground after harvest. They fed the soil peanut hulls, cornstalks, and hundreds of tons of ground rocks, manures, composted materials, and industrial wastes. They took off fewer crops than most farmers, leaving each field to its own recuperative devices one year out of four.

In the early years, they had insects, but these diminished until now they find no more than one variety a year that may need special attention. Yields approximate those of their more chemicalized neighbors, but are less in total because of the fallow year allowed their fields. Over all, the Keenes and their farm have grown into a mutually helpful unit. In a nonexploitive partnership, they feel the satisfaction and the reverence that country folk have felt from time immemorial.

While the Keenes were falling in love with their Elysian fields, they were aware of a growing interest from the outside. First in ones and twos, then in growing numbers, people wrote, or came to see them at work. Visitors wondered if they might buy foodstuffs raised without chemicals or poisonous sprays. The Keenes's process made such elemental sense that people were willing to pay the extra costs of maintaining a healthy soil for its balanced, tasty products.

Their first sale crop was apple butter—Apple Essence—500 quarts the first year. They'd spend whole days in the sun and wind, stirring the bubbling apple pieces in cider in a big black kettle, over a roaring wood fire. Daddy Morgan spelled them off, infant on one arm, stirrer in the other hand.

Soon they shipped out carrots, potatoes, and onions by parcel post, then dressed chickens, eggs in metal containers, honey from their bees, blankets made from wool sheared from their own sheep. Once they crated a live lamb and sent it off. They laboriously ground whole-grain flour and cereal. Later, an electric stone-burr mill and other refinements, including a walk-in refrigerated storage room for perishable grains and flour helped their business.

All the time they were remodeling the chicken house, the horse stable, and the big barn. Now a nice variety of buildings houses their growing business of milling, storing, and merchandising of whole foods. Faithful, understanding, and friendly customers now number tens of thousands. Some come to the Walnut Acres farm store; others order by mail.

The Keenes were among the first to enter the natural foods business. Their name is now well known in America and in some places abroad. They did not plan this—originally they just wanted to get away from that infertile crescent stretching from Boston to Richmond, to live simply and quietly, raising their family in a typical, conservative rural society. But they found themselves caught up in a wider movement. They would have felt remiss not to have given it the best they had.

The farm now includes over five hundred acres. Friends and neighbors work together in unity and fellowship to produce a great variety of quality foods. They grow, harvest, store, grind, bake, roast, toast, combine, can, freeze, package, and ship literally hundreds of good foods. Whole foods from properly prepared soil are prepared in small, labor-intensive batches, daily or weekly. Perishable foods are sent the day the orders arrive—no storage in jobbers' warehouses or on grocers' shelves. At no time are any

of the thousands of commonly used synthetics or preservatives introduced. Every ingredient is listed on each label. In every case for every
purpose, from seed to consumer, the Keenes have sought the best.

Thousands of letters come, telling what better, whole foods have
meant to individuals and families. Occasionally, second-generation
Walnut Acres–fed children have visited, and the Keenes are cheered by
their bloom, awareness, and alertness. A great responsibility, a tremen-
dous possibility, and a rare and heart-warming privilege it is to see the
results of one's effort in living human beings.

Walnut Acres is not organized into a special community. The
individuals and families that work there live separately from one another
in the rural community of Penns Creek. Walnut Acres does not depend
on special living conditions or philosophical leanings. Its approach to
business affairs could succeed anywhere.

After happily working with Keenes for two years, a person becomes
eligible for membership in Walnut Acres, Incorporated. Five shares of
stock are given to each member annually for twenty years, for a maximum
of 100 shares. The corporation owns the whole enterprise—land,
buildings, equipment, inventory, supplies, formulas, and mailing list.

The worker-stockholders own the business and share in its risks and
successes. The former seem to outweigh the latter, but at the heart of the
daily work are a rightness and fairness that make for genuine happiness
and satisfaction. They say, "It is *our* venture, *our* business. Together we
feed thousands with the best of foods. Our purpose ties us and the
universe into a meaningful whole, in which soil and people cooperate.
We help less-fortunate people, locally and far afield, through our small
Walnut Acres foundation."

The Keenes have wondered sometimes about their growth. They have
not wanted to be so large that they couldn't apply their ideals to all parts
of the work. They feel they are close to the ideal size, allowing the
genuine involvement of all in every aspect. Over the years, they have
fought off growth for growth's sake. Each move, each replacing of hay in
the barn loft with piled-up cartons of canned foods, wrenched their
spirits. They took each step always for what seemed valid reasons.

In the 1970s, people everywhere awoke to an energy crisis—to the fact
that all are earthbound creatures, "that we live fully only as we keep
wholesome, reciprocal contact with the soil." National food manufacturers and chain stores are never slow to sense a bandwagon, nor reluctant
to jump on. It wasn't long before they began dashing about, seeking
supplies of "natural foods."

The Keenes were approached from all directions with million-dollar offers to sell out, with inquiries about expanding enormously with their additional capital; with appeals to manufacture and sell their food through larger companies. These offers were fun for a while, but not in the least tempting. The Keenes simply did not consider upsetting the philosophy and the practice of a lifetime for mere money. They felt somewhat self-righteous during that period—their size felt so good.

Basically, they still think small. They live one day at a time, plant one field at a time, harvest one crop at a time. They've adopted a decentralist or intermediate technology, using slower machines of earlier years. People are at the center. Fields are small, averaging 3 acres; their village is small, with four hundred residents; their church, school, neighborhood groups are small. They have found richness of life in smallness.

Walnut Acres is simply good living on the land. Around them are frugal Amish families on good farms of one or two hundred acres. Through careful planning, hard work, and simple living, the families carry on happily. Because of hills, stones, and small fields, farming there is difficult; topsoil is not deep, and yields may be small. Near Walnut Acres, land is high priced enough so that a young person, without family help, cannot take up farming. When consumer prices are set so that Iowa farmers just make a decent living, Pennsylvania farmers really suffer.

The Keenes say:

> May the day come soon when people everywhere recognize that a first and significant task is making the land available for those who would use it wisely and ordering our world so that millions of families can once more make a satisfying living from the soil. Basically we think small; we feed and plant one small field at a time; our church, school, and neighborhood are small. We're glad for what we learned from Ralph Borsodi about soil and life; we're glad to be part of a circle which knows that small is human, that living soil is the basis of health, and that the Earth abides.

14

Thirty Years at Lane's End Homestead

A SENSE OF worth, dignity, and responsibility is the key to the quality of life in this new age. That is why the Borsodi pattern of modern homesteading appeals to many thoughtful families. No one knows how many have taken this way in the past forty years. No one knows how many have talked with, or read, Ralph Borsodi, or visited his Dogwoods home or the School of Living and then fashioned their own family productive home. No one knows how many chose this pattern without ever having heard of Borsodi. But it is clear that thousands of families have done so. Each such adventure is a story in itself; each warrants a place in a decentralist revolution.

Here we have space to highlight the life and development of only a few. I include three that grew directly from Ralph Borsodi or his School of Living: (1) the Loomis Lane's End Homestead near Brookville, Ohio, where John and I lived from 1940 through 1970; (2) the Bill and Martha Treichler family who maintained a three-generational homestead from their beginning in 1950 at Birch Lake Farm in Iowa to their present New York homestead, now involving fourth-generational little ones; (3) the 35-year-long versatile and "educational" Sonnewald Homestead of Harold and Grace Lefever, near York, Pennsylvania.

Lane's End

When I left the School of Living in the spring of 1940, I returned to Ohio, and as we had planned, John Loomis and I were married. Our Lane's End 30 acres (5 miles south of Brookville, a half-mile off the main road) was the setting for a good life—for John Loomis, his sons, and me—for nearly thirty years.

Seeking improved education for his small motherless sons (and hampered by conditions on his Missouri farm in 1930), John Loomis had come to Dayton, Ohio. There he and I met on the Liberty Homestead. Following the dissolution of that project in 1935, John bought at auction 30 acres with a rundown cottage (the core being an 1830 loghouse) and old barn, and a crumbling tobacco shed for $1,050. Here life brought us a new and vital period, largely guided by the School of Living.

Our first adventure the summer of 1940 was refurbishing the cottage. Visiting friends helped us tear out partitions, remove thin ceiling boards with century-old dust falling on us, exposing sturdy hand-hewn beams. Pine-paneling the walls, adding a glistening copper-hooded fireplace, and sanding oak floors completed a rustic, enjoyable living center.

Neighbors helped us dig a well. We added electrical equipment for grinding flour and cereal, for shredding and juicing and for kneading bread. We planted a half-acre garden, pruned old fruit trees, repaired the chicken house, shops, and barn. In due time, we took down the tobacco shed.

John's pride and joy were his farm animals—his team of Belgians for plowing and haying; his beautiful Jersey cow; several pigs each season; his small flock of sheep, and a flock of chickens. With simple equipment, we farmed the four 7-acre fields and garden. We raised all our grain and all the feed for our animals. Our milk and cheese, eggs and meat, vegetables, peaches, apples, pears and berries all came from the farm.

We produced food first for our own use, and many a year that totaled 95% of all the food we ate. Sale of a small surplus of soybeans, hay, or corn netted about $1,000 cash each year, which covered gasoline for an old Ford, electricity, taxes, and repairs—and sometimes equipment bought at local farm sales.

Modern homesteading was our delight, and it was a puzzlement to our neighbors. Friends and visitors came frequently; local people couldn't understand so much traffic on our lane. "What do people see in farming that just makes ends meet?" they wondered. They did understand our neighboring farm that took prizes every year at the county fair for the highest yields of corn.

Our "old order" neighbor, Howard Brunk, harvested our 7 acres of grain on shares. One day, I met him at the barn gate to take a pan of wheat from the bin of his big machine. I hurried to the kitchen, switched on the electric oven and the small electric mill. Quickly I ground the grain and mixed the eggs, buttermilk, and several cups of the new flour to make a batter to spoon into muffin tins. I popped it in the hot oven, and soon the good odor told me the muffins were browning. I turned them onto a board, buttered several, and went back to meet Howard, approaching on his second round.

"Want to taste this year's crop?" I asked, handing him the little package.

"All ready to eat? It hasn't been half an hour! Umm. Good!" he said, biting into one. "Best I ever ate," he grinned. "And this wheat hasn't been to Minneapolis or Kansas City—or even through the local mill at Prymont."

We talked some about milling grain at home. When he started his tractor, he called with a cheery salute, "Thanks a lot—and congratulations on the homestead way!"

Several Dayton friends asked if their children might spend a week or a month at Lane's End. To accommodate them, we turned the old milkhouse into sleeping and craft quarters. We put in a big window overlooking the creek and built bunks and benches for as many as six children to extend "our family." They helped in the garden, cared for animals, picked berries, hiked in the woods, and particularly enjoyed natural food at our porch meals. Later, when they were teenagers, they'd come back to reminisce about digging potatoes or harnessing Fanny and driving the small wagon around the pasture.

Friends came, too, to discuss our way of life. They arranged to gather informally once a month, as a local School of Living, to examine modern homesteading and decentralism as an alternate "way out" of a cultural decline. They often helped mail our monthly newsletter, *The Interpreter*.

Each spring brought its visitors. In 1949 came Ed Robinson and Lyman Wood from Vermont. Like Borsodi, Robinson had a yen for the country, even as a New York advertising man. He was intrigued with the Suffern, N.Y., School of Living advertising piece, "Have-More Vegetables" and others in the *How to Economize* series. Why not develop a program and really sell these ideas to the public?

With his advertising know-how, Robinson prepared pamphlets on several aspects of homesteading, calling them *The Have-More Plan*. During that pleasant visit at Lane's End, they photographed our activities and gathered data. The story of Lane's End in an early issue of their *Have-More Plan* brought more visitors and correspondents.

People from a distance stopped by or spent vacations at Lane's End. Many a morning we'd find an out-of-state truck or camper in our barnyard, with someone sleeping to await the dawn. One August day in 1950, we couldn't believe our eyes! A real prairie schooner, a covered wagon, with two tethered mules nearby, cropping the grass. Two enthusiastic *Interpreter* readers, June and Farrar Burn, had arrived from Bellingham, Washington. We invited the neighbors over. Farrar regaled us with songs and stories. June told us about her years radioing good nutrition in New York City and about their homesteading on Waldron Island in Puget Sound. They bought their mules and rig to tour the country to see what was happening to people and soils.

They had just discovered William E. Albrecht at the University of Missouri Agricultural School. "He isn't yet, but surely will be soon, recognized as one of America's greats," June said. "His experiments prove the dependence of human health on the health of the soil, plants, and animals." We welcomed and read the books she showed us: Albrecht's *Soil Fertility and Deficiency Disease; Soil Fertility and Sound Teeth; Soil Fertility and Democracy.*

"At age 50, I'm going back to college to get an M.A.—in Soil and Nutrition under Dr. Albrecht," June announced.

A treasured book in our library is *Living High*, June's report of the Burns's glorious partnership with nature, in vagabondage from the machine age and money values. With their lives in their own hands, and with a thin pocketbook, the Burns were uncommonly resourceful and lighthearted.

Lane's End School of Living Building

In the spring of 1950, young Al and Maudie Ebling lived with us. From an eastern city, they hoped someday to build their homestead "out West." Al heard me talk about a School of Living building for guests and apprentices. "Let's start it," he said. "I'll help, and learn a lot, and you'll have more space for your work."

Fine! A paid-up insurance policy netted us $2,000 cash. We planned a 30′ × 30′ room on the ground floor for meetings, with an adjoining two-story 13′ × 30′ section. We built of concrete, hauling sand and gravel in Al's truck from a nearby quarry. We used an electric mixer and poured concrete into a movable, double-wall aluminum form. We had our problems with rain that prevented pouring; days of no electricity when lines were being repaired; a broken concrete mixer; boils on Al's hands when we women worked alone; broken ropes that dislodged beams we were guiding up inclines! But we had satisfactions, too. We celebrated when our first round of concrete stood five inches high. A 6' × 7' pane of glass was discovered in a junk yard for our picture window. And we always appreciated friends who came to help. Chief of these were Larry Labadie from Detroit and Chet Dawson, who had read our newsletter as a GI in the Far North. It was November when these two poured concrete on the topmost round of the second story. To the toast we raised to them that night, Chet rubbed his hands and ruefully responded, "I'm glad I came from Alaska to freeze my fingers for Lane's End School of Living!"

By spring 1951, most of our new building was functioning. In a much-appreciated visit, Ken Kern from Oakhurst, California, installed book shelves and counters for mailing *The Interpreter*.

We decided to memorialize all the love, work, and meaning in this adventure by having a dedication celebration. Again, friends came. Ralph Borsodi was there. Speeches were made, our struggles and mistakes laughed about, wise and serious thoughts expressed. But I was too overwhelmed to hear. What had been open space in our cornfield was now enclosed with four walls and a roof! I climbed a ladder to the highest peak of the roof and nailed a leafy twig to represent the Tree of Life gracing our School of Living.

In the fall of 1951, our young niece Betty, her husband Chuck, and two small children came from the Ozarks to live in our new building. For four years we worked together. Their youngsters grew. Two babies were born, delivered simply and naturally in the pretty, airy bedroom that not long before had been wet concrete. Our friend and Brookville's local physician, Dr. Charles Thomas, attended. A natural birth at home was news in our area. Friends, and friends of friends, heard about it, asking if they could "escape" hospitals and do likewise. In the next five years, seven babies were born naturally in our School of Living building with Dr. Thomas attending.

Conferences and Official Incorporation

Our educational work was part of our life at Lane's End. Our School of Living building was headquarters for editing and mailing *The Green Revolution*. We organized annual regional and national decentralist conferences: at Bloomington, Illinois, in 1946 and 1949; at Troy Mills, Iowa, in 1950; at Earlham College, Richmond, Indiana, in 1951 and

1952; at Wittenberg College, Springfield, Ohio in 1953; in St. Louis in
1954. To them we invited persons in various New Age, alternative
culture groups to lecture and lead discussions, to exhibit their wares and
books. Responding were Joe Nichols of Natural Food Associates, Noah
Alper of the Georgists, Griscom Morgan of Community Service, Edwin
Wilson of the Humanist Association, Daisy Wingfield of the Gesell
money reform, Jonathan Forman of Friends of the Land and Organic
Farming. Teachers of natural childbirth, breast feeding, Montessori,
Steiner and Summerhill education, and many others also attended. The
cross-fertilization of ideas was reported by Robert West Howard of *The
Pathfinder* and *Christian Science Monitor;* by F. H. Behymer of the *St. Louis
Dispatch,* and other national journals in the 1950s.

In 1954, members of our Ohio informal School of Living voted to
become an official nationwide School of Living for adult education. We
applied, and were incorporated, as an educational nonprofit group in
Ohio on 5 July 1954. The charter and by-laws repeated the purpose and
structure of the Borsodi School of Living at Suffern, N.Y., an association
of artists, craftsmen, and teachers to study and teach how to live like
normal (fully-functioning) human beings.

Visitors and apprentices joined in our activities. Among the long-term
apprentices in the 1950s and 1960s were Ray and Lila Russ from Florida
(whose search I reported in *Go Ahead and Live*), Don Werkheiser from
Connecticut, Bruce and Betty Elwell from Philadelphia, Ferdi and Becky
Knoess from Chicago, Robert and Arlen Wilson of New York City. All
worked for and helped edit our journals, *Balanced Living* and *Green
Revolution.*

Letters flowed in and out, asking and answering questions. Particularly
treasured were beautiful hand-scripted approving ones from Lewis Mumford. Authors sent books and pamphlets, and our postmaster suggested we
install a larger mailbox at the end of the lane.

Lane's End Homestead and its School of Living, until John's death in
1968, was our bond with hundreds of Green Revolutionaries.

15

Treichler's Three-Generation Homesteads

BILL TREICHLER, a young veteran of World War II, was challenged by Ralph Borsodi's decentralism. On his family farm in Troy Mills, Iowa, Bill's efforts to incorporate Borsodi's concept of a three-generation family, adapted to a Midwest farm situation, made history in the decentralist revolution.

Bill Treichler had met Borsodi in the 1946 decentralist conference in Bloomington, Illinois. A few years later, courting his bride-to-be, Martha, at Black Mountain College, he suggested she read Borsodi's *Education and Living.*

In the fall of 1948, Bill and Martha arranged for Borsodi to visit their campus. Most of the students had never heard of Borsodi, and they questioned and disagreed with him. But disarmed by his quiet good nature, even hostile students were won by the force of his ideas. Many became admirers. Martha was as enthusiastic as Bill—they decided to develop their own homestead with Bill's parents on Birch Lake Farm.

In 1950, they married and moved in. Bill contributed farm equipment he had bought with his Air Force savings. Their first step was to design and build a home for themselves. Following Borsodi's ideas, their home should have an area for home production—a compact, efficient kitchen with plenty of work-space for food preparation and preservation. Bill's father suggested they make a model, so they could view their home from every angle.

Led and reinforced by what they read in Borsodi's books and the School of Living's monthly *Interpreter,* Martha and Bill built their bricks and glass home, with a pole roof, across the lawn from the main house at the edge of Birch Lake. They skinned poles, dug ditches, cleaned old bricks and laid them up. The senior Treichlers helped, too. Sometimes they sat around the table talking things over, especially when they didn't agree on the next steps. The new house was ready to move into at the end of the year, and by then baby Rachel moved in with them. The Treichler homestead was three-generational.

Bill and Martha were enthusiastic about organic farming, decentralism, and proper nutrition, gleaned from the *Interpreter, Organic Gardening,* and Lady Eve Balfour's *The Living Soil.* Meeting like-minded homesteaders at decentralist conferences greatly stimulated their ideas. The elder Treichlers were tolerant—but not enthusiastic.

In return for Bill and Martha's garden produce, the older Treichlers helped with clothing for the growing children. Grandmother Treichler turned out stylish dresses, shirts, overalls, winter coats, and mittens from adult worn-out garments. She taught Martha to sew, and Rachel too had her sewing lessons from her grandmother.

Bill and Martha's children helped with homestead jobs when they were five and six years old. By ten, they sold strawberries and sweet corn of their own. In the winter they carried wood for fireplace, cookstove, and furnace. They joined the 4-H Club and, from their own garden, exhibited products at the county fair.

Grandfather's standards for children were high. The children enjoyed watching him work, and he encouraged their interest. When the children littered the lawn with old oil drums and boards for shacks, with tricycles and wagons and recent finds from the farm junk pile, the grandparents were often disturbed. The solution was to give the children their own space, sheltered from view by a barn and by trees, where they could build to their hearts' content.

Some serious disagreements came from differences in attitudes about farming as a business. The parents, particularly Mother Treichler, thought the young Treichlers should earn money by farming for products to sell. Bill thought they could earn more by producing their own living on the farm. Martha joined him in wanting to concentrate on being as independent as possible of money.

In the early years of their marriage, they spent only about $5.00 a month on food. The farm supplied all the wheat, corn, milk, butter, cheese, eggs, beef, fruits, and vegetables they needed. Some years, they raised cane for sorghum. The woods supplied firewood and logs to put through their sawmill for building. Later, they sold soybeans, hogs and cattle, whole-wheat flour, and corn meal. In general, they followed two methods—raising as much as they could for their own use and also selling products for cash.

In the 1950s, Bill and Martha kept close contact with friends in the School of Living for support and inspiration for their way of life. To some of their neighbors and nearby friends, self-sufficient homesteading was a retrogression, a return to "horse-and-buggy days." But Bill and Martha shared Borsodi's vision that it was much more—that their homestead was a creative way of living with the advantages of an extended family, and an efficient and human part of a decentralized economy. For them, the School of Living approach was an enjoyable, worthwhile adventure.

In 1954, the Treichlers joined in sponsoring the School of Living conference in their home town, Troy Mills, Iowa, population 950. Nearly all the people in the community had a part in it, listening to Ralph Borsodi interpret the philosophy supporting rural, self-sufficient, three-generational living in the modern day. I described Lane's End Homestead in Ohio. Ralph and Rose Smart brought a film on clothing design. Tim Lefever described his low-cost building with solar heat at Sonnewald Homestead.

Two more children were born at Birch Lake Homestead. They grew on its food, played in its woods, explored its fields and lake. They became close friends with people in the community, and with distant ones who came to visit. Martha was a 4-H leader for five years. They took time to read, study, and make things for their house.

As the children grew, the Treichlers doubled the size of their cottage and still they needed more room. If they invested further in the house, could they buy the farm? But their parents were not ready to sell. And the U.S. Army Corps of Engineers were proposing a dam downstream on the Wapsipinicon that might completely flood their farm. Bill, Martha, and family decided reluctantly to make a change.

Bill applied to be farm manager at the Colorado Rocky Mountain School, and was accepted. The family would stay together in the country, and the children would attend the mountain school. They spent two happy years there before the school phased out its organic farming program.

The Treichlers then moved to a similar school at Vershire, Vermont. They taught as well as looking after the school farm and garden. Four of their five children graduated from Vershire Mountain School; three went on to college. Martha earned an M.A. degree from a nearby college.

When Bill's parents died, Bill and Martha received a cash inheritance. With that, plus savings, Bill's family bought 88 acres on a hilltop in New York's rural lake country. They went homesteading the second time.

They have been happy on the new homestead. Each of the youngsters has projects they had not been able to have until the family again had land of their own. The children have been equipped and trained for this adventure—philosophically, emotionally, materially. The daughters make nearly all their own clothes, including coats. Joe, the oldest boy, also makes some of his own, including a carefully tailored leather jacket and trousers.

Rachel owns all her own tools and office equipment for creative silversmithing and free-lance photography. Two sons, still in college, own hand tools collected at auctions, as well as a new metal lathe and a used crawler-tractor with a backhoe. Eighteen-year-old Barbara works her large antique loom and spinning wheel, a treasured graduation present.

The Treichler family are committed to their second three-generation homestead. On it, the children are assured of help and hospitality. Both parents and children agree on the importance—even necessity—of each person having individual choice and sovereignty within a three-generation family. They look forward to each child using a part of the family homestead to continue the three-generation pattern.

> We agree with Borsodi that one's first need is to assume responsibility for our own survival—to avoid being parasitic. To accept and fulfill our gift of life is integrity.
>
> To be both productive and sovereign calls for land and life in the country. To create something better than ourselves, we need to nourish and foster growth in our children. This is parenthood, our link with the past and the future.
>
> Homesteading integrates both inner forces and external aspects. We have discovered that surviving and living in this way inevitably makes a person compassionate and a creator and admirer of beauty. We recommend three-generational homesteading for a good life.

16

Sonnewald: Self-Sufficiency, Home Industry, and Social Outreach

THE LEFEVER FAMILY'S Sonnewald Homestead near Spring Grove, Pennsylvania, demonstrates other aspects of modern decentralist lifeways. They not only produce 70% to 80% of their food, but instead of selling surplus agricultural products, they earn their cash by two services operated on their homestead. One is Harold's (Tim's) electrical and plumbing repair service; the other is Grace's nutrition and natural food store. Both qualify for the term "cottage industry," now becoming common in decentralist circles.

Sonnewald Homestead merits its name, Sunny Woods. Sixty acres of grassy fields and strips of woods encircle a small pond. At the center is a cluster of several modern buildings where this busy family lives and works. Sonnewald provides for the Lefever family itself, and often for many more guests and apprentices. It is also the setting from which their activities contribute to the wider good of society.

The Lefevers' first goal, and their achievement as well, is a high level of self-sufficiency. Someone works every day of the year mulching, tilling, planting, pruning, feeding, or harvesting in their several acres of orchards, berries, and gardens. Rows of lettuce and endive are planted in early spring and autumn to become summer and winter salads and "green drinks." Sheltered greens and root crops are uncovered and used fresh from under winter snow, or from root cellars. At harvest time, freezers and refrigerators are full of summer fruit and vegetables. Celery, cabbage, mounds of carrots, beets, turnips, potatoes cover the root-cellar floor.

Someone is always busy in the kitchen preparing, processing, or consuming their own good natural food.

There's nothing isolated, withdrawn, or backwoods about Sonnewald Homestead. Almost any day there's a surprising interaction of people, concerns, organizations, movements. From the mail box there's a daily armload of magazines, books, letters. Scores of telephone calls are handled, with conversation and transactions completed while Grace, phone resting on her shoulder, chops salad or puts carrots through the juicer.

Committees meet there several times a month, planning for local, state, and national activities. Visitors arrive daily for consultation on nutrition, solar and wind energy, ecology, organic gardening, composting, civil rights, economic reform, etc. Customers arrive, too, for Tim's plumbing business, or to shop in Grace's health-food and book shop.

A day I spent at Sonnewald is typical. Actually, my day began the night before. Along with many others, I arrived early at the monthly meeting of the York Natural Food and Health Association, of which Tim and Grace were principal officers. Tonight's subject: A World Without Cancer.

Unloading from their station wagon, the five Lefevers carried in boxes and books. Dan and Nancy set up the literature table while Grace and Tim got the meeting underway for a standing-room audience.

The program featured an hour-length film, A World Without Cancer, showing the difference between well-nourished and poorly-nourished human cells. In the latter, toxins and poisons are not eliminated. Decades of excess body-toxins irritate normal cells, and the body responds with an overbalance of estrogen, which further disturbs metabolism and causes uninhibited growth of cells called cancer. The conclusion? That cancer is a deficiency, a degeneration, a disease of civilization, in which packaged, processed, and devitalized food has a prominent part.

In addition, the film showed the effect from the use of vitamin B17, or amygdalin, made from apricot pits. In the body, this extract releases hydrogen-cyanide, which inhibits, arrests, and destroys cancer cells. We saw the vigorous Hunzas in the Himalayas, among whom a case of cancer has never been found—a major item of their diet is apricots.

In the film, dozens of cancer patients were interviewed before and after their use of B17 extract. At the end of the meeting en route to the Lefever homestead, Tim said, "Couldn't get people to start home—it's the latest we've ever been."

"And one of the largest crowds," Dan said. "Nearly a third of them newcomers and first-timers."

"A lot of them took free literature, or bought a book," Nancy added.

"And York's leading physician was there," Grace exulted. "He didn't say anything, but he bought a book on *A World Without Cancer.*"

We tumbled into bed after midnight, and woke to the phone ringing. "Wonderful meeting! Congratulations!" a neighbor greeted Grace. Several times an hour someone called, adding enthusiasm, or asking, "Why haven't we known this before?"

Nancy missed her school bus, and Grace chauffeured her to the village. Harold went off on a schedule of repairs. Grace returned to greet customers at the store. Mark, an apprentice, ground fresh flour, cut beautiful cheese, packed nuts and fruit. Dan plowed out the summer's onions. I picked lima beans and pears for drying. The steady low heat in the drying oven was just right to take the chill from the house until the sun warmed the solar panels on the second floor.

While Grace set out good bread, cheese, and applesauce for lunch and prepared her weekly order for health foods, Tim and I talked of his past, present, and future goals. "Did you grow up on a farm?" I asked him.

"No—our forebears were farmers, but my family lived in York. My roots go back to the French Huguenots; they left us a legacy of resistance to war and tyranny. Our genealogy shows Sonnewald Lefevers as the eleventh-generation descendants of Mengen Lefever, who settled with others in the central Pennsylvania hills."

"What influenced you most as a young person?"

"My father was a mechanic, and I learned his skills, followed his interests, and read all the science and mechanic journals I could find. I was headed for an electrician's apprenticeship. I had no trouble making good grades in school . . ."

"You mean you were first in everything," interrupted Grace, "and finished electrical engineering at Penn State in three and a half years."

"Was that where you got your plan for solar heating your home?"

"No, that came later. But I did get a technical and engineering background. War had been declared when I was ready for a job. Several jobs were available. But all involved war work, and were not compatible with my pacifism. Westinghouse seemed the least objectionable, and I took a job with them in Pittsburgh."

"What did you do when the U.S. entered the war and you had to register for the draft?"

"I registered, but declared my objection to war. They allowed me a conscientious objector's position. But when I was called later, I refused to report to conscientious objector camp. This, of course, was illegal, and I faced prison. In June 1942, Jane and I were married; the next day, officers came and took me off for arraignment, and later to prison for draft refusal. But Jane was a plucky bride, stood it well, and did her part in antiwar education."

"Did your prison years have an impact?" I asked.

"Yes, very special. I made friends with several outstanding conscientious objectors, and came upon a monthly paper, *Brethren Action*, which you, Mildred, and a few Ohio Church of the Brethren people were writing. It was an analysis of war and pacifism, and in advance of the official denomination's position. You were espousing rural life, decentralism, and interpreting Ralph Borsodi's work.

"I studied every copy," he went on. "Still have them filed away. I don't believe anything equals the effect that Borsodi's ideas had on me. They put together what I saw, felt, and believed. From them, I began to be motivated toward self-sufficient and homestead living. Several other fellows in prison also saw the homestead life as consistent with nonviolence and pacifism."

"How and when did you develop Sonnewald Homestead?"

"I bought our 60 acres in 1944, and put up a quonset hut with one all-glass side, facing south—a crude beginning of solar heating. Jane and I lived in it seven years, and our first three children were born there. We lost Jane when the children were little. Grace and I were married a few years later, and we moved into our present solar-heated home."

"Will you explain your solar-heating system? Did you design it?"

"I found a plan in *Popular Science*—one of the earliest discussions of solar heat—designed by Maria Telkes of Massachusetts Institute of Technology. I showed her my adaptations of it, and she approved my using her fundamental design. Basically, it calls for a second story with high, double, or thermopaned windows, facing south, with proper roof overhang that permits maximum use of winter sun, and minimum summer sun. Back of the exposed panels is a thin steel sheet painted black. Enclosing the six-inch chamber behind the steel sheeting is an insulated board wall. The steel sheet is heated when the sun shines, as is the air in the narrow chamber on each side of the steel. Maximum temperature is about 140 degrees. A thermostat on the ground floor regulates the fans which blow warmed air to the first floor. We have had supplementary heat from a heatolator fireplace, now a Franklin stove, and also from a small oil heater. We heat the core of our 65' × 30' house at low cost, entirely satisfactory to our needs."

"How do you rate the cost and energy used for fuel on your homestead?"

"Actually, our fuel bills run only about $100 a year. The ecology department at Dickinson College in Carlisle did a survey of energy used in four homes of comparable size. Our home used the lowest amount of all, while a modern suburban home used almost double, as did a cooperative student house. I figure that, over the years, our family has used as little energy from irreplaceable sources as almost anyone else in the country. It's a good feeling to be part of lightening the burden."

"Any other features of Sonnewald you'd rank as important as your solar heating?"

"I think our compost heap belongs there. That big area of leaves breaking down may not be the most scientifically layered compost, but it is always ready for mulching our trees, berries, and gardens, as well as being tilled into the soil. They're hauled here each year by the York Street Department, and we're glad to pay the small cost for each firmly pressed load of many tons."

"What influenced you to do all that?"

"Long ago, we were inspired by the way the Chinese had kept soil fertile for four thousand years. They used every bit of vegetable waste. All that leaf mold has helped Sonnewald in that direction for over thirty years. Our soil grows increasingly organic."

"And with all this, you've also been active with the School of Living," I exclaimed.

"Having been influenced by Borsodi and you, Mildred, at Lane's End in the beginning, we followed that pattern. We're listed as one of the 'centers' of the School of Living. We've been members and often officers of the school since the early 1940s. I've been president of the board of trustees several times, and Grace has been chairman too. The whole family attends the school's conferences, and we helped move the school's headquarters from Ohio to the East in the 1960s."

"Are your summer conferences part of the School of Living program?"

"Yes, several times each summer, a group of forty people studies and shares our activities for a three-day weekend. People appreciate it, and along with volleyball, swimming, and folk games, we all have a good time. We must have had five hundred people over the last five years—we continually hear of the homesteads those people have developed all over the states, and the community action they're doing."

"Now what about those four mobile homes on the slope beyond the orchard?"

"They might suggest a trailer court, but actually they help Sonnewald express a very old and basic principle of the School of Living good-life concept—that of the expanded and three-generation family. Those trailers have made it possible for my parents and older aunts and uncles to live here with us. They helped care for the babies and youngsters, and our children have been glad to have Grandpa and Grandma close by. They and the children would shell peas, string beans, make Christmas decorations, go on bird walks. And we helped care for them when they were sick, we shared their lives, and mourned their deaths when they left us."

"A far cry from an old people's home!" I remarked.

"Yes—I agree with Borsodi when he says the family probably came into existence to care for the elderly as much as to care for children," Tim replied.

"And your adolescents—how does Sonnewald appeal to them?"

"We and they look upon youth as a time for venturing out of the home nest, but returning to it at any time of need. Our children have followed this pattern. The boys have married quite early—Bart and his bride lived with us for a while, and Evan and Sharon are back now, helping me with windmill research, and building a new storage barn. Willa is traveling, and right now is in an Iowa commune. We'll all enjoy having her back home when she arrives."

Tim excused himself. "A job needs doing before I leave for a meeting of the Pennsylvania Organic Farmer/Consumer Organization in Harrisburg."

Nancy came in from school, fixed herself a sprout-and-tomato sandwich, and began preparing the main dish for supper—a mammoth bowl of cut greens, beets, carrots, and cucumbers.

"Have you a plan for yourself when you are out of school?" I asked her.

"Yes, I want to be a teacher."

"So, you have some teacher whom you admire and want to be like?" I guessed.

"Yes, my Mom," she replied.

In a day noted for its generation gap, Nancy's reply testifies to the success of the Sonnewald Homestead. Many visitors, apprentices, and third-generation residents value their experience there. They are aware of lacks, problems, and imbalances. Some find it strenuous, others find it hectic. But the benefits are clear.

When others are threatened by shortages, the Lefevers have more than enough. When energy is being wasted, they are heated by the sun and powered by the wind. When people are weak and sick, they have no need for doctors and nurses. When others are lonely and deprived, they enjoy family, neighbors, friends. When others are apathetic or helpless, they are interacting almost daily with important groups for social change in civil rights, war resisters, natural foods, the Church of the Brethren, Georgists, ecologists, the School of Living and its land trusts. When millions trek to monotonous jobs in factories and offices, the Lefevers work creatively at their own pace on their own homestead.

Several hundred customers keep a lively business going in the Sonnewald Food Store, stocked with whole grains, dried fruits, and natural vitamins. It would be hard to find a better demonstration of the postindustrial decentralist revolution than Lefever's Sonnewald Homestead.

17

Peter van Dresser: Planning for a Decentralist Future

Energy Planning

In THE EARLY School of Living days, 1936–40, Peter van Dresser was a frequent and welcome participant. A creative architect and engineer by profession, he was giving thought to strategic and emerging decentralist technology. His cogent analyses and recommendations often appeared in the decentralist journal *Free America*. So clearly did van Dresser predict the energy crisis and outline alternatives that his comments were republished verbatim years later (1975), by *Mother Earth News*.

For a decade, Peter van Dresser lived on a homestead in Florida, and in 1949 he moved to the New Mexican Rockies to "integrate with a deeply-rooted local community, and to grow with that community, rather than start a brand-new intentional society, or to demonstrate a largely illusory self-sufficiency." Through the years, he has continued writing and giving counsel.

As far back as 1938, in "Technics of Decentralization," van Dresser pointed out that we were in a power age rather than in an industrial age. He emphasized the centralizing effect of stationary coal-steam power. He pointed to the decrease and approaching exhaustion of petroleum reserves. Since the manufacture of automobiles—the greatest power age industry and keystone of our economic structure—is dependent on this supply, drastic reorganization in both our technology and economy is necessary. Almost 95% of the mechanical power in the United States is used in transportation, and most of that in trucks and automobiles. The power age is also a transportation age.

The answers predicted in 1938 by Peter van Dresser for the petroleum shortage included extracting oil from shale, an increasing use of coal, the harnessing of all available waterpower, and the production of alcohol from crops as an alternative fuel, along with power from the wind, tides, the sun, and geothermal sources. Even these would not be altogether adequate, he said. Synthesized oil or alcohol would be more costly than oil from gushers; coal would be harder to come by; all the falling waters in the country would meet only a fraction of the current energy needs; wind power is not adaptable to many industrial uses.

Peter van Dresser predicted that to power consumption would be added the question, "Is power doing work which needs to be done at all?" Could it be eliminated under an economic arrangement more logical than finance capitalism? Why should railroads proudly reveal that the average potato travels 741 miles from the field to the corner grocery? For railroads, this may be a good thing—but it is a very bad thing for an efficient use of coal and mineral resources.

Like Ralph Borsodi, van Dresser emphasized local production-and-use of many goods, and the decentralization of social practices. Much of the horsepower used in transportation would be unnecessary in a de-centralized and well-rounded regional development. The ultimately practical solution of the power problem lies in decentralizing America.

Hydroelectricity is almost the lifeblood of the modern trend toward decentralization and a life-technic economy. It breaks down the old coal-and-steam concentrations of factories and populations. Electricity dis-tributes power over wire through the countryside, facilitating con-servation; a mine often blights a countryside. Small dams, properly engineered and constructed, can control floods, drought, erosion.

Wind-driven electric plants are best adapted to light-industrial or domestic use, and are an important part of a distributist-decentralist technology.

In many ways, alcohol is superior to gasoline—it burns more cleanly, is adapted to high compression, with less heat loss. When the rising cost of petroleum puts the cost of gasoline one-third more than alcohol distilled from starch crops, it will make alcohol feasible. Since it is dependent on farming, not mining, for its crude material, alcohol production would push the economy toward an agrarian (though not necessarily de-centralized) operation. Solar heat will be used to run steam engines, operate refrigerating units, and generate gas for cooking. Its most practical use is in heating domestic water.

Arthur Pound said in 1936, "The most important business of mankind has been putting power, more power, and ever more power, behind wheels for increasing convenience and prosperity of society." Peter van

Dresser calls this attitude the *infancy* rather than the wisdom, of science.

Short of the use of atomic energy (which would be an absolute major catastrophe) van Dresser said, "We shall be forced by natural laws to revise our attitude toward machines, energy, and power. We shall be forced to develop a kind of technic closely related to the natural cycles of land, water, air, and living matter—applied more judiciously and efficiently than is done today." But there is no lack of supply. America's farming lands can supply not less than 7½ billions of horsepower. More and more technics must refine this titanic laboratory, and fewer and fewer concern themselves with an attack on the bowels of the earth and ever-more-powerful contrivances.

Community Planning

As we enter the uncertain 1980s, Peter van Dresser supports the relative independence of families on modern homesteads but deplores the concept that evolved to almost a "cult of primitive self-sufficiency." Among the 1960 "communiteers," many young people held notions of flight to the wilderness and a return to a new tribalism and to the womb of "mother earth."

In their New Mexico center near Santa Fe, Peter and Florence van Dresser encountered increasing numbers of dropouts from psychedelic enclaves in San Francisco, New York, and their various megalopolitan suburbs, who were trying to live out these fantasies. While sympathetic with their unhappiness with the financial/industrial "establishment," and their desires for an alternative life-style, van Dresser could not disregard the fumbling, fragmented, and often self-defeating qualities of their efforts to achieve such an alternative.

Particularly in contrasting these efforts with the patient continuity of the Old Mexico villages in the region, van Dresser became aware of the inadequacy of the one-track, do-it-yourself each-in-his-own-bag approaches of many of the new "pioneers." Van Dresser noted that "this cast of mind seemed to predominate even the communes where people appeared banded together more in mutual hostility to the square world, with a grudging minimum of cooperation among themselves for bare survival, rather than a generous sense of mutual humanity."

This sort of *reductio ad absurdum* of the earlier concepts of American independence and self-reliance seemed to van Dresser to be hindering rather than aiding evolution toward a more-balanced ecologically-viable society. Even a simple economy requires a degree of specialization and organization in order to achieve necessary technology. The hardiest pioneer cannot mine, refine, and forge the iron for his axe. Fragmented individuals cannot achieve this degree of social structure.

Soon after settling in a several-hundred-year-old village of Spanish-speaking people in the Southwest, van Dresser realized that "the strategic kind of pioneering needed at this time was in terms of community, not of individual survival and self-reliance. Even a degree of community self-reliance, at most partial and relative, must be balanced with a wholesome exchange and relationship with the locality, the region, and the world."

For such reasons, van Dresser began to think that the restorative process needed in our society could be better called "recentralization" rather than "decentralization," but recentralization on a scale compatible with real human needs and with the facts of energy and conservation of natural resources.

Peter and Florence van Dresser, as immigrants into a new land, decided to integrate with a deeply rooted local community, to grow and evolve with that community, rather than to start a new project. This proved to be a "long, slow, and unspectacular process, with its successes modest, diffused, and often ambiguous, with many and repeated frustrations."

A large part of their effort was the prosaic business of working out a means of livelihood that meshed reasonably well with, and enriched, the local economy. In their case, this was primarily a small village restaurant, using food that was personally, locally, and regionally produced. This included some aspects of the classical homesteading pattern, in that they built homes and other buildings after learning the native techniques. They also raised some of their own food and gathered fuel wood in the nearby National Forest.

They cooperated with villagers constructing the local water system, helped with the irrigation ditches, and participated in a community school. From time to time, "higher level" activities were called for, such as serving on state advisory committees for various development and improvement programs.

In recent years, as one of the founding members of the New Mexico Solar Energy Association, van Dresser has promoted low technology, or folk-level use of solar energy in the region. The small solar house he built in 1958 in Santa Fe is now rated the second-oldest continually functioning solar residence in the United States.

He has participated in a number of seminars on rural and solar development, and has written two important books: A *Landscape for Humans* and *Homegrown Sundwellings*. These are constructive contributions to decentralist and biotechnic development in this and other parts of the world. Peter van Dresser now senses a rootedness and a belonging in a beautiful part of the country which, in this day and age, is not easy to come by.

18

Ken Kern: Little David Among Giant Builders

KEN KERN OF Oakhurst, California, is another life member of the School of Living. For more than twenty-five years he has lived and breathed life-oriented technology. He has designed and built several homes for his family; he has designed and helped in the building of hundreds of other homes and homesteads. He does not encounter any piece of land that his imagination does not immediately see on it people and animals, houses and buildings to fit the landscape, gardens and woodlots to build the soil, and all manner of new cost-saving decentralist technology such as indoor greenhouses, original housing units, fireplaces, and compost privies.

Next to the food industry, building and construction is the largest of all modern industries. Government, corporate, and contractor building have flashed to become giant enterprises. Yet many Americans retain their do-it-yourself attitudes and dream of building their own homes.

Through his books, *Owner-Built Home* (1961) and *Owner-Built Homestead* (1972), Ken Kern has influenced many builders. For thirty years, he has been the little David contending with building Goliaths. His life has a Horatio Alger flavor.

In his student days at the University of Oregon (1947–50), Ken was guided by Dr. Ernest Guyon to a decentralist owner-built philosophy. He left college imbued with creating his own home and homestead from scratch. Hitchhiking down the Pacific Coast in 1950, Ken was given a lift by Morgan Harris, then professor of economics at Chapman College. Their exchange of views revealed a common concern in, and understanding of, the importance of decentralization.

Morgan said to him, "Ken, you belong in the School of Living, founded by Ralph Borsodi. You should read its journal, *The Interpreter.*" Thus began a correspondence uninterrupted to this day between Ken Kern and myself.

In 1952, Ken bought 20 acres of open land in the low Sierras near Oakhurst, California, for $600. He built temporary but artistic shelter and began developing the land, designing and constructing his unconventional housing, and homesteading. He married, and his growing family added incentive, help, and satisfaction to his life's work.

Ken's first visit to Lane's End Homestead was in 1952, when he added hours of work to the School of Living building. He wrote items—always appreciated by readers of the school's journals. The School of Living published his first reports, which he later compiled and republished as *The Owner-Built Home*. His philosophy, methods, and achievements were constant stimulation.

As the disaffection with industrialism increased in the 1950s and 1960s, *Mother Earth News* came on the scene. It republished Kern's *Owner-Built Home*, and a bulge developed in his outreach. He set up his own publishing business on his homestead, and there prepared and published Owner-Builder Publications. To find isolation for his work, the Kerns sought a retreat to a lesser-known spot. Reports indicate annual sales of Owner-Builder books have grown to tens of thousands of dollars; Scribners asked to republish *Owner-Built Home* in a hardcover edition.

In the summer of 1975, Ken published, in collaboration with Rob Thnallon and Ted Kogan, *The Code: Politics of Building Your Own Home*. It is a dynamic presentation of what is wrong with, and what can be done about, injustices in building regulations as they affect owner-builders. Of 200 pages, 40 show homes built by owners outside code regulations. In Mendocino County, California, six hundred such homes provide adequate shelter for the families who built them.

Ever inventing and improving, Ken and Barbara Kern in 1977 bought 80 open acres for a new life-centered laboratory in home building. On it, they plan to construct demonstration homesteads with buildings of wood, stone, concrete, and adobe; with gardens and outbuildings, embodying the best features of the various methods they have discovered over the years.

Ken Kern has become an innovative, popular builder and successful author. His future seems unlimited. But Ken Kern has always been, and will remain, a good homesteader, a thorough decentralist, and a supporter of the American dream of independent owner-built homes. His work for the idea of owner-built homes has struck a responsive chord. As he has written,

> Human beings are complex creatures with physical, emotional, and intellectual needs and capacities. Living in, and

building, their homes should satisfy these needs and develop these capacities. None of these owner-needs is expressed in factory-produced housing, and only impersonally in contractor-built units at excessive cost. No one can create a house fulfilling a person's total environmental needs better than the persons who live in that environment. An owner-built home can join site and ecology; can express one's own concept of aesthetics and design; can facilitate one's own particular life-style, and use available, native energy, resources, and materials.

19

Small Community: Bryn Gweled

A VISIBLE AND viable movement toward creating new "intentional communities," and to maintaining and improving existing villages and small towns, is under way in America. Following in the footsteps of some of the community-building decentralists mentioned in earlier chapters, this movement will retain and revive some of the simplicity and naturalness of the normal way of living for human beings.

Two 20th-century Americans made a special contribution to the building of community—Ralph Borsodi and Arthur E. Morgan. Each established an organization through which to build and improve human community—the School of Living and Community Service, Inc. Both men, and their organizational co-workers, brought standards and resources to add strength and stature to village-community life. Their community goals, methods, and achievements are part of America's decentralist revolution.

Communities are not casual or impulsive groupings. These new intentional communities are willing to observe and study the nature of true community, to instill in them good human relationships and the new institutional arrangements needed for today's world. The influence of Borsodi and Morgan was to include as well ethical land tenure, just and fair financing, and the use of both individual and cooperative effort with a minimum of legal force (i.e., government). Their communities continue into the 1980s, testimony to their vision and determination.

I describe the Bryn Gweled community, a direct outgrowth of Ralph Borsodi's work, and introduce Dr. Arthur E. Morgan and Community Service, Inc., of Yellow Springs, Ohio.

Bryn Gweled Community—Hill of Vision

Bryn Gweled, a community of 77 families totaling 350 persons, flourishes on the northwest edge of Philadelphia. It is historically tied to the 1933 Dayton Liberty Homesteads and the influence of Ralph Borsodi.

Georgia Snyder and I were among the Columbia University degree-seekers who "discovered" Ralph Borsodi in 1932. In 1934, Georgia married Herbert Bergstrom and, with him, directed Bedford Community Center in Philadelphia's ghetto. I had gone to similar social work in Chicago. But in a few years, our enthusiasm for "club work" and finding jobs for the unemployed was waning. In 1939, I was assisting the Borsodis at the School of Living in Suffern, N.Y., and the Bergstroms came to visit.

They were entranced with the productive homestead community at Suffern. They immediately wanted to do something similar near Philadelphia. "Where do we begin?" they asked.

"With study and planning," Borsodi replied.

The Bergstroms and co-workers returned many a weekend for reading and discussion on land-site, land-tenure, raising funds, educating candidates on building and homesteading, and related issues. They recruited others, many of them staff persons in the American Friends Service Committee. With them, they formed a homestead association, and for two years they met regularly to study, plan, and prepare for this move to the good life and social change. In 1940, 240 desirable acres became available to them, and a fund was ready for a down payment. Then followed an adventure in community building and living that still rewards and stimulates its residents.

Bryn Gweled's member-families hold their land in common, but each family has its own lot for its home and buildings. They are Quakers, Catholics, Jews. Perhaps a third are blacks. Their membership includes contractors, lawyers, teachers, engineers, artists, business people, social workers, a tool designer, editors. Most families have children; some have grown, married, and settled down in the community on plots of their own.

Capital funds for the homesteads, including cost of land, roads, installation of utilities, and the community center building, were raised through certificates of indebtedness bearing 3% interest. Capitalization has always been conservative, and most of the money has come from members themselves. Land assessment paid by each homesteader began at, and remains, $12 a month. This sum is applied toward a general budget that covers local taxes on land, interest on debts, and repayment of the capital investment.

Bryn Gweled folks handle community chores with "work parties." Each family is expected to give about one day a month in community work. They dig ditches for underground placement of telephone and electric cables. They built a community center and a swimming pool. They maintain trash and poison-plant control with work parties. The economy of getting work done without paid help is important, but more important is the building of unity and the taking on of responsibility for one's own community. They continue to aid each other with tasks such as roofing and gardening. Most families did much of the construction on their own homes. Many families have large gardens, for "homestead" is not merely a euphonious title—homesteads are productive homes.

Of Bryn Gweled's 240 acres, 80 are reserved as common for roads, woods, and recreation. The balance is 81 family leaseholds of about 2 acres each, leased out for a 99-year renewable term. Each family builds and finances a house suited to its needs, and owns the house but not the land. If a member takes out a mortgage, Bryn Gweled joins in signing, reserving the right to contribute payments in case a family defaults. Because the land is not owned, and because the house cannot be sold to nonmembers, Bryn Gweled is attractive only to those who expect to be permanent residents.

The Plot Plan Committee explains to new members, and their architect, if any, the few requirements on distances between lot boundaries, structures, well, and septic-tank systems. Their neighbors are consulted so that major features will be acceptable. Each homeowner plants and builds as he or she wishes, ranging from natural cover to extensive lawns and landscaping. Though the homes are within short distances of each other, none is visible to its neighbors.

Considerable spontaneous and some organized social life goes on. The community house and playground, tennis court and swimming pool are much used. There are groups who play recorders, sing, square dance, study nature, sew, view films, play and watch sports, or visit around an open fire. The Community and the Children's committees direct community-wide events—picnics, covered-dish suppers, plays, and special occasions.

Bryn Gweled's residents also participate in the civic and social life at the nearby village of Southampton, holding positions on the school board, library board, zoning commission, and in township government. Others participate in Southampton's churches, political and social groups, Boy Scouts, PTA, and Volunteer Fire Company. Bryn Gweled's teenagers edit a popular weekly, *Vox Gweledorum*.

In the 1980s, persons who constitute Bryn Gweled Community are realizing goals set thirty-some years ago. They look on the past with joy and to the future with anticipation. They do, indeed, warrant their community's name, Bryn Gweled—Welsh for "Hill of Vision."

20

Arthur E. Morgan and Community Service, Inc.

ARTHUR E. MORGAN lived from 1878 to 1975. His long life, integrity, quality, and diversity of achievement made him an extraordinary decentralist. He is another, who, without a college education, found wisdom from his own search and experience.

Arthur Morgan and his wife Lucy and three children (Ernest, Frances, and Griscom) lived quietly in Yellow Springs, Ohio. Yet they made of this small town a center for seekers and educators far and near. The Morgans have been unceasingly part of the healthful, simpler, and more real concerns of living.

In 1913, a disastrous flood hit Ohio's lower Miami River area. Dayton's central business district was under twelve feet of water, and the lowlands for miles were inundated. Hundreds of people lost their lives, and millions of dollars worth of property was destroyed. Arthur Morgan had studied, and he had previously written a book, *The Drainage of the St. Francis Valley in Arkansas.* He was asked to assess the Dayton situation, and later he was appointed head of the reconstruction of the Miami Valley. He arranged for spanning five small river valleys converging at Dayton with five huge earth dams. These dams required earth-moving equal to that in the Panama Canal construction. As a magnificent testimony to Arthur Morgan's success, these five dams still block off the streams into wide-spreading conservancy lakes.

A few years later, when Antioch College was seeking a new president, the trustees honored Arthur Morgan with the task. He remained president from 1920 until 1936. One of his important contributions at Antioch was the initiation of the work-study cooperative plan, in which students spend a period studying on the campus and follow it with a period at work in the larger world.

In 1933, President Franklin D. Roosevelt invited Dr. Morgan to become chairman of the Tennessee Valley Authority. The TVA was even then a big operation, with millions of dollars to spend and with several thousand people employed. Stupendous physical and engineering feats had to be successfully confronted.

At the same time, however, Arthur Morgan saw his co-workers succumb to dishonesty, chicanery, rivalry, misuse of funds, and the abuse of authority. He deplored the absence of basic integrity. As he reflected on the causes of, and decline in, the personal character of so many individuals, he came to some significant conclusions.

In *The Long Road*, he pointed up the cultural roots of immorality. It stems, he said, from modern "specialization"—a lack of diversity, a turning from solving many difficulties in life, especially in youth. He raised questions about the mechanical and scientific complications of the modern world, and the helplessness we face when our telephone or radio is out of order, or when a town needs a new bridge, or when our roses develop a new malady. Morgan preferred a road steering away from specialized doctors, financiers, chemists, and educators—to find a culture in something larger, namely, a developed human being. He saw the roots for a human culture in "good homes and small communities." So Morgan left the TVA to return to Yellow Springs, there to devote his life to that small town and other small towns like it.

Dr. Morgan's next step was "to strengthen the small community in America." His family joined him in 1940 to establish Community Service, Inc., to counsel people in developing intentional communities and in improving the nature and quality of existing small towns. With this, of course, he faced the implications of technology, of attitudes, and of philosophical grounds. The alternative that Community Service sought to present was that of the small organic community:

> Because most people are unaware of the essential part which the intimate community must play in human affairs, and do not fully realize the implications of the disintegration of community life now under way, Community Service undertakes to increase knowledge of community life and concern for it. Those who see the limiting and depressing qualities of small community life seldom have the vision of what a good community can be, how it can meet the fundamental needs and cravings of a human spirit. Community Service seeks to clarify a vision of community and to help many people to share it, so that work for community betterment shall not consist of patchwork efforts, but shall lead to the fulfillment of a truly great concept of community life.

Griscom Morgan and his wife Jane developed their own homestead in the Vale Community, to foster an experimental intentional community with its own mother-taught children's school. Ernest Morgan developed a family-owned business in bookplates, and later he and his wife assisted in Celo Community, near Burnsville, North Carolina.

Celo is a cooperative landholding community with title to land in a homesteaders' association which leases land to the members. There now are nearly one hundred members who have developed a variety of small-scale enterprises—a book-publishing company, a memorial burial society, and the Arthur Morgan School for Children, free of regimentation.

In many ways, Yellow Springs responded to the Morgan influence. Citizens took part in town planning, not so much to increase the size of their town as to improve the people's health and well-being and to improve the town's appearance. A community forest with its now-famous Glen Helen has an outdoor-education center and well-developed trails for nature study. The Fels Laboratory carries on child-care research in Yellow Springs. Many Antioch College students find a model and challenge in their college town.

Griscom and Jane Morgan, plus others, are staff members of Community Service, counseling community builders, publishing books, pamphlets, and a bimonthly newsletter. They hold an annual conference and maintain an excellent library and book service. Among their titles is their own excellent *Guidebook for Intentional Communities*.

"A good community will not be invented, discovered, or 'just grow,'" said Dr. Morgan in 1975, when he was 97 years old. "It must be forged from the purpose and quality of the lives of people living in it."

Community Service, Inc., has brought significance to thousands of small communities in America. It has interpreted their part in the "small, molecular, moral forces" which change cultural patterns.

21

The Community Land Trust

SINCE HENRY GEORGE'S great *Progress and Poverty*, the "land problem" has received a great deal of attention. A chief hurdle to any widespread movement of families to country homesteads (as well as to other kinds of decentralization) is the high and rising cost of land. Ralph Borsodi was twice a prime mover in initiating a new form of land tenure for homesteading communities. It was known as the 999 lease in Dayton's Liberty Homesteads, and as the indenture plan in the School of Living Bayard Lane Community. Similar programs are both necessary and anticipated, if decentralization is to proceed noticeably. Community land trust programs are an important step in that direction.

In Borsodi's lifetime, this new land-tenure program surfaced again in 1966 through the cooperation with another decentralist, Robert Swann. During World War II, Swann was in prison for conscientious objection to war. In a group of COs, there was study of the newly forming decentralist movement. They followed a study course developed by Ralph Templin, then director of the School of Living. Their texts were Arthur Morgan's *The Small Community* and Borsodi's *Flight from the City, This Ugly Civilization,* and *Prosperity and Security.* Outstanding in this study was the way the School of Living communities held land in trust, each member-family leasing from the community and not selling the land as private property. This impressed Robert Swann and since 1945 this idea has occupied a large place in his thinking.

In the late 1940s, Robert married, and he and his wife Marjorie were active in the peace and civil rights movements. Both of them saw decentralism consistent with, and necessary to, nonviolence, as perceived by Mohandas K. Gandhi.

Robert Swann was carpenter, designer, and builder of houses. In two cooperatively owned enterprises (in his home town, Yellow Springs, Ohio, and in Kalamazoo, Michigan) he learned how crucial land values are to low-cost housing. In 1956, he joined Morris Milgram in the first racially integrated housing in Philadelphia. Again, he saw how much land value and site value hamper successful housing. More time and money are spent by builders in the United States in locating suitable land than in actual supervision and building.

Both Marjorie and Robert Swann realized that speculation in land and natural resources is a root cause of a great deal of injustice and, therefore, violence. For their life base, the Swanns developed in 1960 the CNVA Farm (Committee for Non-Violent Action) in Voluntown, Connecticut. They organized it as a trust, with community-held land. They urged the peace movement to augment picketing, protest marches, boycotts, and civil disobedience with decentralization and removing land from private exploitation and profit.

Most nonviolent activists, according to Swann, tended toward either socialism or anarchism, neither well defined nor articulated. Most pacifists disclaimed socialism as practiced, but seemed to find no other term to describe their essentially humanistic economics and politics. Swann found Borsodi's thinking and action rigorous in examining all aspects of life. In his view, Borsodi's courage in maintaining that economics must deal with moral issues refreshingly contrasted with the timidity of most well-known economists. He decided to tie in with Borsodi.

In the mid-1960s, Robert Swann was working in the civil rights movement in the South—rebuilding burned-out churches in Mississippi. Seeing the landlessness, the helplessness of the black population, Swann saw their need to get on land of their own. He learned that Ralph Borsodi had just returned from four years in India, and had similar ideas for *world* development.

In India, Borsodi had had long conferences with leaders of the Gramdan movement, particularly Jayaprakash Narayan, who, as a follower of Vinoba Bhave, had become a prominent leader. In 1953, Narayan gave up his post in the cabinet (and probably his prime ministership) to join Vinoba Bhave, then walking through the villages of India, asking for land to be put in trusteeship under the Gramdan village control of all land. When Borsodi met with Narayan in 1966, the Gramdan movement included thousands of villages and affected the lives of millions of people.

Borsodi recognized Gramdan as similar to the hopes and plans he had presented in Dayton and the Suffern School of Living communities. In Gramdan and Narayan were a power and a force that needed to spread around the world as an alternative to the centralist methods of communism, socialism, and state capitalism. In India, the Gandhian heritage and organization provided Narayan a following of millions. In

America, the pseudo-economics of Keynesianism and the "affluent society" made serious consideration of Borsodi's ideas difficult.

Ralph Borsodi and Robert Swann joined forces. The two men put their energies into forming a nonnational agency to revitalize rural areas throughout the world. In 1967, with the help of R. E. Dewey of the University of New Hampshire, Gordon Lameyer of Bradford College, and myself from the School of Living, the International Independence Institute was launched for this purpose.

Persons from any part of the world may become members, depositors, and investors in the International Independence Institute (III), a nonprofit cooperative registered in Luxemburg, whose main purpose is to teach, sponsor, and assist the formation of community land trusts.

The Community Land Trust is a legal entity, a quasi-public body, chartered under state laws to hold land in stewardship for all mankind. It is administered by a board of trustees, some of whom may live on trust land, but (to insure wider interest and community responsibility) 50% of the trustees do not. The community land trust implements holding of land for the common good; it is not primarily concerned with common ownership.

The trustees of a trust secure land by gift or purchase and then declare (and hold) it nonsalable. They arrange trust agreements (contracts) with those who will use the land constructively and who, instead of a purchase price, pay an annual rental to the trust equal to the economic rent of the land. Out of this fund, the trust pays the county and state land taxes. Land users build, own, sell, and use the buildings and labor products on the land as their own private property.

Having returned to the South with land-trust agreements, Robert Swann found southern leaders understanding and approving. He met Slater King, a relative of Martin Luther King; a real estate dealer; and a civil-rights leader in Albany, Georgia. In spite of discrimination problems, Slater King was helping the poor get land of their own. He saw the land trust as an equitable and just method of holding land, and a way by which blacks could not be thrown off their land because of ignorance or white chicanery.

Slater King and Swann arranged for a group of southern leaders to go to Israel to study the Jewish National Fund, one of the oldest, largest, and most successful land-trust arrangements in the world. Israelis had held land in trust since 1890, when the first Zionists came to Palestine and bought land from absentee Arab landlords.

Heads of seven influential groups in the South who made the trip to Israel included Faye Bennett, executive secretary of the National

Sharecroppers Fund; Slater and Marion King; Charles Sherrod, officer of the Student Nonviolent Coordinating Committee (SNCC); Albert Turner of the Southern Christian Leadership Council; Lewis Black of the Southwest Alabama Farmers' Cooperative Association; Leonard Smith, a regional director of the National Sharecroppers Fund; and Swann, as head of the International Independence Institute. That such a group of leaders could be assembled in a short time indicates the welcome for the trust idea, and at the same time each group constituted avenues for effective spreading of the idea.

From their study and tour of Israel, these leaders recommended the land trust to their constituents. Conferences were held in several places, and action was taken in 1969. In the spring, New Communities, Inc., was formed to operate as III's first land trust. An option was taken on 4,800 acres near Albany, Georgia.

Financing (over $1,000,000) came from trust membership, as well as from religious denominations, governmental and educational groups. Officers and members of New Communities Trust were blacks and whites, as were applicants for family homesteads on trust acreage. The plan combined private homesteads on some land and cooperative farming of other areas—an adaptation of the moshav in Israel. Families lived on their 5-acre homesteads via lifetime lease of the land from New Communities, and held private ownership of improvements. They could earn additional money by cooperative farming on some of the trust acres. Other earnings in the cooperative went to develop the entire community.

The significance of the International Independence Institute lay not only in achieving the nearly 5,000-acre Albany trust, but in being an agency for continuing such projects elsewhere. Here, for the first time in U.S. history, was an open, voluntary agency, one of whose primary purposes was to achieve land reform in the framework of liberty and security, stemming from America's unique economist-philosophers Henry George and Ralph Borsodi.

Word spread of the Independence Institute and its work. Calls came from other trust developers for III's help and supervision. To serve all inquirers, in 1972 the III published a handbook, The Community Land Trust: A Guide to a New Land Tenure in America. Part I defines the concept and discusses its application and political dimensions. Foreign and American models in actual use are described, and the process of incorporation is outlined. Part II deals with the organization, structure, land selection, financing, land use, and social planning. Included are how to determine rent, the matters of taxation, zoning and codes, as well as duplicates of actual lease contracts in use, replicas of eight actual land-trust contracts; the early School of Living "Indenture for the Possession of Land," "Contract for Lease of a Farm under the Jewish National Fund," the Voluntown Peace Trust, the New Communities Trust, incorporation and by-laws of Bryn Gweled Homesteads, and others.

Robert Swann travels widely by invitation and to conferences on trust action—to Europe, South America, Mexico. Successful land trusts formed in Puerto Rico and Mexico provide alternative land systems to the owner-tenant relationship on sugar, coffee, and cotton plantations.

In the United States, a growing youth movement in the 1970s was seeking "community on the land." Many young people, generally ethical and nonmaterialistic in outlook, welcomed the justice implicit in the community land trust. Counterculture media swept the term into prominence, and it is now much discussed.

Special journals appeared to espouse land reform and give space to community land trusts. Outstanding are *The Maine Land Advocate* (Orono, Maine) and *People and Land* (San Francisco). Among the hundred community land trusts operating in the United States are Northern California Trust, a function of a Coalition for Land Reform; the Evergreen Land Trust in Washington State; and the Sam Ely Trust (Brunswick, Maine) working toward a regional trust to include much of the land in Maine. In Madison, Wisconsin, a School of Living member, Bruce Allison, is working with a group to put a large area of southeastern Wisconsin into a regional land trust.

In 1976, the School of Living incorporated into a trust the land of some of its centers. Increasing its own trust and guiding other community land trust developers is a major emphasis of the School of Living.

The American dream—family maintenance and economic freedom— cannot be achieved in the milieu of high land costs, mortgages, foreclosures, and taxes. Individuals and families, by themselves, are tied to the treadmill of working and saving, only to see their resources dwindle because of inflation, high cost of food and transportation, and especially the increasing cost of living space through rent and price of land.

At a time when human use and misuse of the earth is a matter of vital concern, the Community Land Trust not only affords a ready instrument for the protection of land and the husbanding of its resources for future generations, but it also enables persons to effect significant changes in social policy in the face of apparent governmental lethargy.

As a way to lessen exploitation and to lower and eliminate the cost of land, the community land trust is an urgent and significant aspect of the decentralist revolution.

22

Constant Currency

ELIMINATION OF THE land monopoly through community land trusts is not enough. There is a second important problem that had occupied the individualist anarchists: money. Eliminating monopolies in credit, money, banking, and the issuing and redeeming of currency is a necessary step in the decentralization of America.

Ever-increasing inflation and rising prices of goods plague the average American family, both causing, and resulting from, unbalanced federal budgets, and the government's printing of money. One government administration follows another continuing a dishonest money system and increasing the federal deficit. So common is the unbalanced federal budget that it has come to be accepted as "the American way."

Actually, an unbalanced annual budget of the U.S. government did not appear until 1950. In 1800, the federal budget was $11 million; the tax burden was $2 per individual, and the national debt (after a long Revolutionary War) was $83 million. But the *annual* federal budget was in surplus. By 1900, the national budget had soared to $521 million, the tax burden per person to $7, and the total national debt to $1.4 billion. But still, the budget was in surplus.

It took a century and a half (from 1800 to 1950) for the national government to accumulate its first $250 billion of debt. In the next three decades (1950–80), the U.S. Treasury more than tripled the level of debt accumulated in the previous 150 years. By the early 1980s the annual budget outlay was $602 billion; the per capita tax burden well over $2,000; with the nation's debt headed toward $1 trillion, and the budget in deficit almost $70 billion! This rising level of treasury debt represents only the accumulated cash deficit of the government in Washington. It does not include the debt of state or municipal governments (or the various agencies within them, like sewer authorities and school boards).

The federal budget deficit is simply what politicians in Washington spend over and above the taxes they collect from citizens in cash. In three years (1975–78), the U.S. government increased its debt more than in the three decades 1945–75—years of the Korean War, the Vietnam catastrophe, and the Great Society's New Frontier.

To a decentralist revolutionary, the national debt represents loss of national independence, just as a personal growing debt to one's banker suggests increasing dependence on him. In 1968, the interest on the national debt was $15.4 billion; in January 1977, it had risen to $40.7 billion. The interest on the federal debt is now almost 40% of all money spent on the Western world's largest military establishment—and that is larger than the annual cost of all schools, colleges, and education.

Rich American citizens own much of the national debt in the form of treasury bonds and government securities. Middle-class Americans are paying interest to them. Serious as that is, it is worse that the foreign ownership of the U.S. government debt has risen sharply. In December 1939, it was $200,000; in December 1976, over $100 billion! Eighty percent of this debt is readily marketable whenever those foreign governments and individuals choose to cash it in. On this international level, governments and empires are made and broken! This process of foreign indebtedness accompanied the disintegration of the British Empire. In 1977, the International Monetary Fund again rescued the collapsing British pound with a $4-billion loan. The pound sterling collapsed because Arab oil sheiks and other foreigners decided to sell their large holdings of British government debt securities for dollars, marks, yen, and Swiss francs. A century of British budgetary deficits had caused this loss of confidence. A once-stable Britain was prostrate before former vassals and the Middle Eastern oil bankers, now the owners of the British national debt.

The inescapable point is that America, too, is losing its independence to foreign bankers. The hard-earned taxes of U.S. working people are being transferred to foreigners to pay the interest and principal on the national debt which foreigners own. We are transferring an even larger part of this total debt itself to foreign creditors. We are mortgaging the republic to strangers and governments over whom we have no control, and of whose loyalty we can never be sure. The pervasive and irresponsible momentum of federal government expenditures is to make the United States an increasingly insolvent and illogical debtor.

The course of any debt-ridden individual or institution is loss of personal freedom. When a national government spends more than it taxes (and borrows from its own rich citizens and rich foreigners), that nation not only impoverishes its working people by taxing them to pay the interest, but such a nation will, in the end, forfeit its sovereignty.

Debt-ridden citizens increasingly lose their freedom and their self-esteem. Debt-ridden nations lose their sovereign independence.

An Honest Money System: Constant Currency

Ralph Borsodi had long been aware of the complex, serious financial difficulties in the United States and the world. He understood not only the operations of the existing money system (relatively rare even among public leaders, not to mention the average citizen). Borsodi was confident of the fundamentals of an honest, stable system of banking and currency. He had outlined and called for such a plan in 1943 in his *Inflation Is Coming!*

Inflation did come, not as rapidly nor to a crescendo of runaway proportions as Borsodi had predicted. Such dramatic inflation was forestalled by government acceptance of Keynesian-controlled inflation, with increasing government regulation of prices and the market. Americans have escaped (so far) the catastrophe of *runaway* inflation, but at increasing loss of liberty. Ralph Borsodi could not believe that liberty-loving Americans would tolerate such extensive government controls of industry and prices as they did in the quarter-century following 1943.

With alarm, Borsodi watched the world's financial crisis deepen in 1972. Troubled, but not surprised, he read in the newspapers in March 1972, that President Nixon had devalued the dollar. Theft and robbery, Borsodi called it—the reduction of value in the people's savings by 25%, a regressive tax levied on people without their participation, understanding, or consent.

What should he do? Decentralist revolutionary that he was, Borsodi believed that government has no place in administering or controlling money. Government should only set standards for money—as it does in weights and measures. Government should not operate banks or issue money. Banks should be cooperatives of depositors. Commercial banks should issue money, backed by actual goods going to market.

Borsodi could write another book—repeat what he had presented in earlier books, elaborate the cause and cure of inflation. "But the world has had enough words—plenty of books on money reform have been read, set aside, and forgotten. What is needed," he decided, "is an experiment, a *demonstration* of an honest, stable currency. Real people in an actual community could and should print and circulate their own money—operating their own banking system."

Ralph Borsodi realized the challenge of such a proposal; he foresaw the hurdles and obstacles. "Money reform is the most difficult of all necessary social changes," he admitted, "but second only to land reform is urgency for a decentralist revolution."

Borsodi decided to act—to start a new, people's money, to experiment in his own hometown and state. Since 1974, Borsodi had lived in Exeter, New Hampshire, a typical New England small town, a good place (eutopia) of some 2,500 people. He explained his plan to Exeter bankers and some businessmen. They were willing to cooperate. Several hundred friends and neighbors became investors in a new nonprofit cooperative corporation, the International Foundation for Independence, to operate an ethical money system, as the International Institute for Independence had brought an ethical land system into being.

The International Foundation for Independence was different—it was cooperative and voluntary, instead of governmental; it was world-wide, registered in Luxemburg; it would issue money with a new standard and backing. Certainly its money would not be tied to government debt. It would not be based on one commodity—gold—as some money experts proposed. (History had proved that the price of gold is too fluctuating, dependent as it is on the uncertain discovery and supply of gold.) The new money would be based on, and backed by, a select number, or "basket," of 30 staple commodities, such as silver, gold, aluminum, zinc, lead, tin, wheat, oats, rye, soybeans, sugar, peanuts, rice, coal, iron, and oil. Checklike notes were printed in various amounts, called "Constants." Each Constant was equal to 20 cents; five Constants equaled one dollar. Quantities of commodities in which the Constant could be redeemed were listed on the back of each one.

This particular basket of commodities represents an accurate cross-section of the basic elements of the world economy. Since inflation, almost by definition, expresses itself as a rise in the average prices of such commodities, a currency based on holdings of such commodities would have a stable constant relationship to them, and thus to prices in general. While the price of one or two commodities might drop in the world market, it is not likely that all would. Thus a fluctuation *within* the basket would not seriously affect the *whole*. The issuing corporation, IFI, is obligated to maintain one such basket of commodity holdings for each 50,000 Constants in circulation, and to redeem them in kind, on demand. Thus, unlike the U.S. government, the IFI could not just print more Constants than it had commodities. Thus, its currency was not inflatable.

Robert Swann assumed the directorship of the International Foundation for Independence to take the Constant into a larger-than-local test. He would supervise the nature and weight of the commodities in the basket, or index, which backed the money. He would assemble a fund of capital large enough to move into the commodity "futures" market.

This futures market of staple commodities on the international level would involve the purchase and sale *on the same day,* to take advantage of differing price levels at different spots on the globe. Known as "arbitrage," this buying and selling on the same day would not be speculation. Speculation is the deliberate holding of goods off the market for some time, in anticipation of a price rise. Arbitrage would involve the buying of wheat in Egypt, and selling it at a fraction of a cent more per pound in London, on the same day. In this way, arbitrage would facilitate trade, rather than hinder it, as does speculation.

The experiment with Constants operated for more than a year in Exeter, N.H., and its surrounding territory. It was reported and described in *Forbes* magazine, *Business Week, Financial World,* the *Boston Globe,* and other newspapers. It demonstrated the structure and operation of an honest money system. It developed a fund for loaning to small-scale enterprises, particularly in the Third World, at reasonable (5%, 7%, and 10%) rates of interest. (In many Third World countries, particularly India, money lenders charge 33% to 50% interest on loaned money.)

A very interesting experiment in the use of both the community land trust and the idea of a commodity-backed-currency is the one currently being developed by Robert Swann near Great Barrington, Massachusetts. Swann proposes that some form of locally produced *energy* be the unit of measurement and the reserve currency for redemption purposes.

In looking for a universal form of money, obviously the most sought-after forms of fossil fuel energy are poorly distributed and limited in supply. An energy form is needed that is both renewable and universally available. Robert Swann proposes that some convenient measure of wood energy become the standard unit of measure for currency, and also its base for redemption. He suggests a plan for a local, but universal, money and banking system.

Structure for this system would come from a group of organizations such as cooperatives, community development corporations, community land trusts, local merchants, and small businesses. Although not actually forming a bank, they could operate through a local bank. Deposits in the bank would be in terms of U.S. dollars initially and it would make loans for increasing local self-reliance in food, energy, and housing. Such a proposal has already been initated in the southern Berkshire region in western Massachusetts. The surplus could be invested in energy commodities—a good source is forest or trees—or directly in cords of wood, under a community land trust. As the supply of cord wood from the forest becomes available, each depositor would then be issued a certificate or note measuring the value of his or her deposit in energy or in cords of wood if one chose to redeem it.

The group of organizations could then "issue" or provide credit for projects of real productive value within the local community, and would no longer be entirely dependent on U.S. dollars. Thus a new approach to money could begin—with not only local but universal value in a world economy, no longer dependent upon or tied to the nation state and its vast bureaucracies.

23

Evolving Persons: Creating a Mutual Society

DECENTRALISTS HAVE MOVED into the 1980s with optimism.

Yet there are serious problems to face—for example, the economic and political roots of injustice and oppression. But in addition to changes that must be made in "the system," we know that individuals must change—that we must evolve into the kind of human being that we say is ideal, not the kind that the society of the 20th century has generally produced.

The centuries-old "sense of sin" is being replaced by newer knowledge of the human self. Modern psychologists—Erich Fromm, Carl Rogers, Rollo May, A. H. Maslow—report that the human personality is rooted in dynamic, positive, and growing energy. Persons are moving, becoming, growing toward maturity—entities discovering a true self and developing latent potential. Better knowledge of inner states—of one's self—mean less disturbance by anxieties, fears, or pessimism. Self-actualizing persons can see life more objectively, can have clearer perceptions of cause and effect, can establish friendly relationships easily, and are rarely, if ever, exploitative.

One hastens to admit that ignorance and misery persist, that millions lack psychological insight and skills. Yet there is a growing confidence in confronting these problems. Genius and help in self-actualizing come from many sources. Here I present three examples from the decentralist ranks whose psychological expertise is not a specialty but a part of an integrated life approach. One is Joseph Chilton Pearce, a former humanities teacher, with his revealing analysis of brain development. Second is Donald Werkheiser, former editor of the *Journal of Human Relations*, who is articulating the maturing process via evolutionary psychology. True and Clear Marks, trainers in self-community-growing are my third example. Each adds strength and ability to human development and a positive outlook.

The Magical Child

In his book *The Magical Child,* Joseph Chilton Pearce, four times a grandfather, developed his findings from new discoveries in physics, significant brain-neural research, and careful observation of infants. People learn, he says, by advancing naturally from one matrix to another. A matrix is a situation in which there is a source of life, energy to explore, and a safe place in which to explore. A mother's womb is a crucial matrix, where growth stages are genetically coded from three billion years of preparation. To block or disturb these stages interrupts and distorts growth.

Between the eighth and twelfth week, fetal brains explode in activity. Brain cells in close proximity communicate; preliminary interaction and random learning take place. In the fifth month of pregnancy a marvelous ordering begins. Cells differentiate according to function; optical cells align into nerves that carry messages from the eyes; aural cells from the ears, etc. The brain begins to function, to learn from that which is outside. New research proves that the infant in utero is a living, responsive, intelligent creature. We must reevaluate our notions of learning, perhaps of speech itself, and our notion that an infant is an undifferentiated organism.

When proper gestation is complete, the infant's body releases hormones triggering the birth-delivery system. The mother's body picks up these hormones, and re-stimulates the infant—a continuing back and forth to insure efficient delivery. "Never again in life," says Dr. Pearce, "will intelligence have to make such an extreme and sudden adaptation and learning as that involved in being born into the world."

Even when all goes well, birth is a potential trauma for this highly intelligent infant. With a brain system five times larger than its body, it knows a primal fear of lack of oxygen. As the infant's body drops into the birth canal, it releases large quantities of the hormone ACTH, increasing protein in the liver and brain. This is vital to the new learning at hand. In turn, the body releases more adrenalin (which adults experience when startled) and organizes the body for its great survival maneuver. The body responds: Toes point back, fists clench, the back arches. This brief physical passage is not without hazards. Birth stress is a key to the physical bonding with the mother—an instinctual genetic response; and birth stress prepares the brain for massive new learning. This learning and this stress are key to the bonding between the mother and child on which all development depends.

Dr. Pearce's facts on the bonding of human infants with mothers are crucial and significant. Bonding is a nonverbal, psychological communication—an intuitive rapport beyond ordinary rational thinking and perceiving. It is genetically built into human beings. The mother is built to respond to her infant at birth, and the infant is built to expect it. Bonding seems to involve specific hormones, and breast feeding is a crucial factor in establishing it. In societies where bonding is general, infant crying is rare. Ugandan children operating from a bonded matrix are calm, happy, and enormously intelligent.

Birth is a significant matrix. The mother bond and the brain's processing of sensory information at breast feeding is likewise crucial. Moving on to later matrices rests on the success of these earlier experiences. New experiences must have sufficient similarity to the known. If the earlier biological plan is interrupted, then there is no way of relating the new to the old. Confusion results and learning is impaired.

Dr. Pearce reports the error—crime against nature—in modern mechanized births and in the crude inattention to a child's natural learning processes. The unbonded person spends his life in search for what bonding was designed to give. His intelligence cannot unfold because it does not get beyond this primal need. (Witness the child with his blanket—tragic symbol of our defeat and his substitute for mother's touch.) The cruelty of abandoning infants at birth does have its "reward": Development is slow and retarded. We clamor for fame, "things," consumer goods.

Technological birthings and child rejection are root causes of interpersonal breakdown. They are root causes also of our modern obsession for material things. But awareness of this problem can produce a turnaround in education: "Stop the telling; the human being from birth on is a natural learner; let it learn, answer its questions, and learn with it." A return to sanity and intelligence is possible from the growing attention to, and revival of, natural birth, breast feeding, and bonded child care.

Evolving You

What more can be done, for and with the faulty body-minds who now constitute our adult population? Although some persons have given up, and drown their search in drugs or pleasure, many others offer programs for educating and retraining feelings, values, and behavior. One who believes that human beings can evolve into levels not generally produced by the 20th century is Don Werkheiser, former editor of the *Journal of Human Relations*. He is an analyst of modern exploitative authoritarian relationships, with solutions and suggestions for a society of mutualism.

As a young man, Werkheiser was critical of both education and modern business, for both, he felt, transgressed his concept of freedom as a primary human need. He chose to earn his living as a carpenter. His concern for liberty led to his friendship with two outstanding libertarian thinkers and writers—Dr. Theodore Schroeder and Laurence Labadie.

Dr. Schroeder had developed theories of evolutionary psychology and the scientific maturing of human emotions. His prolific writings describing the emotional compulsion resulting in dominance/submission and love/hate helped interpret the behavior of power-seeking politicians and monopoly industrialists.

Laurence Labadie, son of Detroit's gentle anarchist of the 1900s, Joe Labadie (secretary to Benjamin Tucker), was heir to the books and writings of Josiah Warren, Stephen Pearl Andrews, Lysander Spooner, and Benjamin Tucker. In associating with Labadie, Werkheiser had contact with one of America's ablest interpreters of the early challengers of America's monopoly system.

In the late 1950s, Werkheiser came to the Lane's End School of Living, where he assisted in editing and writing the School's journal, *A Way Out*. His discussions there with Laurence Labadie and Ralph Borsodi, who also visited from time to time, were long and deep. He heard me speak of Henry George, and John Loomis spoke of LaFollette's "progressivism." On one point we all agreed: that the generally accepted economic-and-political patterns were operating primarily for the benefit of, and under the control of, certain beneficiaries, to the disadvantage of other persons.

Don Werkheiser's writings call this condition "single-convenience relationships." Any organism, including a human being, acts in such a way that favorable consequences occur. The producing action thus is reinforced. This is "single-convenience," for the effect on other things or beings is not considered. If this unilateral condition becomes conscious and is pursued successfully in human relationships, one is subordinate to the convenience of the other. The superordinant operates at his own discretion, with his own reinforcing imperatives, to produce those results most favorable to himself. The subordinant does not—he may be

Evolutionary Personality Growth Chart
by Don Werkheiser, author of Evolving You

Personality is defined as an energy system which develops *naturally*, under proper conditions through four evolving stages, with specific types of behavior considered normal for each stage in a life cycle. Unfavor-

Normal Development	Usual Symptoms of Energy at This Stage
I INFANCY 0-3 YEARS	Total dependence on adults. Gives no service for service; does not distinguish self from others. Feelings and wishes are infant's emotional reality.
II CHILDHOOD 3-11 YEARS	Begins to be aware of one's own needs. Crudely aware of others. Prefers own age group. Abundant physical energy; sense of taste, touch, handling predominate.
III ADOLESCENCE 12-18 YEARS	Special effort to relate to the opposite sex; preoccupied with sensations. Idealistic; ambivalent—wants independence, yet is still dependent.
IV POST-ADOLESCENCE BEYOND 18 TO DEATH	Uses senses to get information to better deal with environment; such as taste for wholesome food, sound for adequate communication, sex for reproduction and health.

STEPS FOR RENEWING GROWTH

1. Observe and honestly admit tendency to act on feelings about facts instead of facts. Recognize your own infantile tendencies; your occasional feelings of helplessness; your fear of others and their domination. Recognize your own mature and realistic abilities.

2. Notice your relating to others on your own terms for approval, self-aggrandizement; get rich while others remain poor. Try to see two sides to every human situation; love-hate, inferiority-superiority; sacred-sinful sex.

able conditioning factors may prevent development into the next stage, in which case energy is fixed at the lower stage, and adult energy-behavior is expressed at the level at which growth stopped. Through appropriate steps, however, an immature adult can renew the emotional growth process.

Types of Experience Which Cause Fixation at This Stage	An Adult Manifests His Energy at His Level of Development Stage Not Outgrown
Parents do not lovingly meet child's dependent needs—they scold, neglect, punish, reject the child; insist on performance.	Adult infantilism. Getting something for nothing; gambling, charity, doles, unearned income via rent, interest, profit. Fantasy feelings prevent objectively dealing with facts.
Parents administer punishment for showing off; fail to provide for and interpret new experience.	Adult childishness. Sense indulgence and showing off become ends in themselves. Preoccupied with food, drink, tobacco, drugs, clothes, cars, ostentation, fame, prizes, publicity, power, title.
Flow from inadequate relationship with parent. Parents afraid of or preoccupied with sex. Cultural sex attitudes hypocritical and confusing; control through guilt-inducing religious doctrines, sadistic laws, supernatural threats.	Adult adolescence. Sex and sensuousness become ends in themselves. Preoccupied with sex, sex stories, or over-denial of sex. Depends on novelty, art for art's sake, music, etc., to exclusion of dealing with real situations.
Integrates information and action in ever wider scope in space and time.	Post-adolescent maturing. Knows his own emotional history and the roots of any conflict impulses. Uses rational faculties for acting on real situations. Considers more and more relevant facts.

3. Separate eroticism from reproduction. Then cultivate eroticism without compulsiveness. Maintain responsibility toward reproduction—conceive no child unless willing to be responsible for it.

4. Study general systems philosophy and scientific thinking, and apply to the whole of life. Study anthropology to note similarity of human beings; how differences bring conflict with others.

excluded, exploited, oppressed, denied, or used according to the convenience of the superordinant. This means that—whether it occurs in a democratic or a totalitarian society—one person is the instrument of the other.

Werkheiser shows that modern Western society is single-convenience related, and that "single-option relationships"—SOR for short—predominate.

The task of all persons of good will, we felt at Lane's End, was to change a society so that each person freely decided his involvement with others. John Loomis and I regarded land monopoly as the starkest evidence of single-option relationships. Labadie and Werkheiser insisted it was banking/money. Ralph Borsodi said both and even others were equally SOR.

Werkheiser believes that to eliminate social problems arising from single-option relationships, human beings must evolve and move toward mutual option. This will happen as humans analyze their situation, reassert individual integrity, emerge from the mass, and take action individually and in voluntary groups to improve their relationships.

What is needed, Werkheiser said, is to create "mutual-option relationships" (MOR).

In SOR society, authority is mandatory. In a MOR society, authority is advisory—advice can be accepted or rejected. It is important to distinguish between these two styles, rather than to reject all authority *per se*, Werkheiser points out.

Werkheiser's unique contribution comes from his clarifying of the evolutionary stages, from infancy to advanced adulthood, through which the individual grows—or becomes fixed. He identifies the maturing stages as infantile, childish, adolescent, and adult. This is illustrated in the accompanying chart.

Werkheiser believes human potential will not be realized until a MOR society is reachieved. He notes that just as the potential of chimpanzees was not suspected until they were studied in their natural habitat, so the full potential of human beings cannot be apprehended until they live in *their* natural habitat—a mutual-operation society.

He outlines a maturing process through which people outgrow living "by and for their feelings as ends in themselves." Many factors augur hope. Energetic, healthy adults on more and more family homesteads, with a clear concept of a mutual society, can evolve and mature to give promise that in the continuing struggle between liberty and authority, decentralism will continue and one day will predominate.

Friendly Shared Powers

True and Clear Marks, past middle age, have spent their lives imagining and working for ways to rid the world of compulsion, oppression, hierarchy, hostility, and all the negatives in the psychology books. Their *Friendly Shared Powers* is an important transformational manual that brings individuals back into society in a hopeful manner. "Even in mass society (where people rarely care for one another) we can grow (if we train ourselves) in responsive friendships, in developing effective groups, community self government; and a network of growing systems for justice and peace all over the globe."

In *Friendly Shared Powers* the Markses discuss how to increase self-reliance and friendship. They comprehend what a healthy self, a healthy friendship, and a healthy community are. They locate the dimensions we all can grow in. Then they tackle growing in self-wisdom, by habits that "free" us from controls by locating what we *really* want and that enable us to go about getting it. "Wow!" you'll say. "If we practiced such freeing habits we'd have less need for defeating 'hang-ups.'"

Each page of their book and each hour of one of their seminars develops strong, clarifying concepts. As a reader or participant you learn what steps to take that go beyond yourself and yet also help to change yourself. If you have the wits and commitment to *do* something, you will go about taking those steps. And you will have changed a bit; you will have grown a bit—sometimes a whole lot! Think of the effect of doing this a hundred times a year, twice a week. Think how the world would improve if every community, every village, every neighborhood had such a "growing-up action group" in it.

A decentralist America will continue to develop as people decide to change. The people discussed in this chapter offer some suggestions for how we and our communities can evolve further.

WELCOME TO THE WHOLE WORLD COMMUNITY!

a proposed statement of community purpose and principles.

DEFINITION	A society of people becomes a *community* by organizing a friendly voluntary membership with unifying values, shared concern for the whole body, and shared powers.
PURPOSE	To enhance our lives, freedoms, relationships, livelihoods, and environment, we individuals want to organize communities. Whenever government agencies with weapons or corporations with centralized economic powers threaten aggression, domination, or exploitation, we want to empower networks of local, regional and global communities to act for our survival and mutual freeing. Also we want to organize for community access to land and to other resources we depend on.
1st Principle— PARTICIPATION	We want to practice optimum participation to make community agreements wisely, harmoniously, and creatively. WISELY with determination to enhance the global environment's fitness for healthy life in our generation and in future generations also. HARMONIOUSLY by deliberating with efficient consensus procedures among members, and by informing and consulting concerned nonmembers so they can consent to our agreements. CREATIVELY by allowing any proposal for community agreement to become more creative through members adding friendly amendments.
2nd Principle— FREEDOM	We want nonconsentors to community agreements to feel free for self-directed behavior unless a community finds their actions harmful to members or harmful to the community as a whole. DISCIPLINING OF FREEDOM: We want some community-centered groups to experiment for gentlest adequate preventives of harmful behaviors—nonpunitive but sufficient. RECOGNIZING PRIORITIES: When misbehaving corporations and governments threaten us more than misguided persons, then we expect to put first things first.

3rd Principle— RESPONSIBILITY	To learn to inform, organize, strengthen, and encourage community actions for survival, freedoms, and mutual benefits, we expect to work in small community-centered groups.
DISPOSING OF PROPOSALS	For optimum participation, form small circles. Allow time for clarifying questions. For speediest decisions, choose either to approve, amend, reject, or refer. To improve wording, offer a friendly amendment.

Friendly Shared Powers for Life on Earth: Practicing Wise Habits & Group Genius in Society-Healing Actions
© 1979—Clear Marks
2219 Grant Street
Berkeley, CA 94703

24

We Encounter Decentralists:
A Summary and Challenge

A FOURTH AMERICAN revolution is in process—a decentralist revolution firmly rooted in the basic, freedom-loving, decision-making nature of human beings. Persons, ideas, and activities are included in these pages because they use and fulfill those essential human aspects. In at least four ways, these activities provide what earlier American political, racial, and industrial revolutions neglected or failed to supply.

First, decentralist life-ways are in harmony with nature. The "discovery" of North America was a heady business, giving the colonizers reason for thinking that man had assumed command and was thus fulfilling God's will. Rather than live in harmony with the beautiful land they found, as did the other residents of North America, they assumed that the great expanse of the continent had been preserved especially for them to develop, manage, and exploit. The colonists had to work out the relationship of human beings to government and outlined it in the U.S. Constitution. But nowhere in the original papers of the United States of America is there reference to the relationship of human beings to land and nature.

Americans concentrated on exploration and exploitation. Science and technology produced tools that made war seem inevitable. Giant machines, factories, and cities were not only goals, but became realities. Now, for the first time in two hundred years, the participants in Western civilization had to think seriously about their place in nature. Modern homesteaders, whose lives by choice have been based on the land, are examples of people who live by and rejoice in the harmony of nature.

Decentralists have always emphasized the need to correct two great errors in the American outlook: the way land is possessed and the way money is issued. Again, no principle or counsel in those crucial matters is in the nation's original documents. The U.S. Constitution guarantees the right to life, liberty, and the pursuit of happiness, but contains no guarantee to land. In *Agrarian Justice*, Thomas Paine championed this right to be included. "Not the earth itself, only the improvements on it can be treated as property to be bought and sold," Paine declared. Yet legalized private property in land became an ingrained American custom, with its long train of speculation, maldistribution of wealth, poverty, and conflict. School of Living decentralists countered this age-long error with community land trusts, recognizing land as the heritage of all, granting rights to occupy to those who use it.

Government retains the right to print and issue money for wars, for payment of national debt, and for other nonproductive use. The resulting unlimited inflation robs workers, consumers, and the savers of money, through continuous rises in prices. Decentralists offer noninflationary currency in cooperative, voluntary, local associations.

The units of organization in a fourth, postindustrial revolution are small. Decentralists heed Ralph Borsodi's recommendations to keep units of production, ownership, control, education, government, and population small enough to allow persons involved to meet face-to-face, to know the facts, to really understand and to deal with the issues at hand.

When cultural affairs are operating on the above three principles—in harmony with nature, removing land and money monopoly, and people-control in small local groups—*then* voluntary action replaces coercion, and *then* "the state will wither away." When land is free or available at low cost, when money is stable and credit inexpensive, each individual in a free market will receive what he has earned, none will have what he did not produce, and all persons can follow their inclination for a lifeway. As an invitation and challenge to a creative, human life-style, we have described homesteads and homesteading; people using natural instead of drug healing; people implementing appropriate technology and cooperative, voluntary associations, and carrying on education for living suited to both children and adults.

Although Americans live longer, have more wealth and education than at any time during the century, America ranks first in the world in murder. Violent crime against people and property has tripled in the last two decades. The annual rate of divorce and annulment has more than doubled. Although Americans spend more time in school, the practical knowledge of educated persons has declined. Less than half can complete income-tax and insurance forms without help.

With more free time, fewer work-days, and lowered-age retirement, three out of ten say their favorite pastime is watching television. This adds up to something less than an age of the quality-minded.

On a recent auto trip from the East to Mid-America, we quite unexpectedly encountered decentralists at almost every stop. One evening, we stopped in New Lebanon, Ohio, with a couple old enough to have retired to their rocking chairs. Instead, they are active homesteaders. They served us a cool green drink of comfrey and edible weeds blended in apple juice. (The green drink was made famous by Dr. N. W. Walker, 103 years old, who with a young wife was parent to three children, the youngest 21 months.) A delightful supper of their own fresh steamed vegetables and raw salad was followed by inspection of their garden, lush with rows of twelve different vegetables, herbs, and flowers. The next day, we visited our hostess's father, over 90 years old—he, too, was in his garden, collecting greens for his daily potion. Hale and hearty, he maintained his home and was president of the local natural food club. Hundreds of motorists pass by his garden, unmindful of this meaningful aspect of a decentralist movement—a healthy, aged man, satisfied with his lot, and in no need of help other than from his family.

Hundreds of thousands of Americans are decentralists who don't know they are—they have little if any conscious philosophy of decentralism, but if queried, would say they prefer health to disease, voluntary action to governmental control, fair return for their labor rather than economic injustice, small rather than large cities, and country life rather than urban penthouses or tenements.

It would be well if more and more people better understood and could articulate the principles and practices of decentralization. It is the modern version of the early American dream of liberty. But because of weaknesses and faults in "the American way," champions of opposite philosophies on the Left and Right make their claims known. American citizens are being enticed into the ideologies and practices of fascism and governmental types of socialism and communism. One reason for this book is to assist both demonstration and articulation of decentralization as a way to both liberty and security.

To one who sees the need, range, and implications of decentralism, the current American scene—in spite of a general characteristic of bigness—is hopeful. Evidence of decentralism appears daily, without our even searching for it. For example, the November 1980 issue of the *Leading Edge Bulletin* reports that an analysis of grassroots activity reveals a major restructuring going on in this society. It quotes John Naisbitt of *The Trend Report*, who says, "The single most dominant trend we find in our research is rapid and extensive decentralization." But there is still a long way to go; America has been so centralized for so long. Even in that milieu, decentralists are confident. With William James, they say, they "are done with big things, big institutions, and big success. They are for those small, invisible, moral forces which, like the oozing of water, if given time, will rend the hardest monuments of man's pride."

To those who claim "there is not enough time left" to allow nonviolent, persuasive forces to win, the answer comes: "In employing decentralist forces we create stability and *extend* our time." The choices are clear, and increasingly persons are choosing decentralist alternatives.

> Each worthy cause for a future glorious
> By quietly growing becomes victorious,
> A cause can neither be lost nor stayed
> Which takes the course of what Truth has made,
> And is not trusting in walls and towers
> But slowly grows from seeds to flowers.
> —Kr. Ostergaard,
> *A World of Song*

APPENDIX
A Decentralist Manifesto

A NEW WORLD is being born.

If this new world is to be a better world than the one now dying and to make possible a fuller fruition of the human spirit, then it will be very different from the capitalist world of today, different from the world that the dictators of Russia and China are providing, and different from the socialist world into which most of the world is now drifting.

Concerned and thoughtful men and women are challenged to arrest the present drift into a mechanized barbarism. They want to contribute to the birth of a world in which persons will be free to realize their potentialities as creative beings. Such leaders must have the courage to assert themselves and must discipline themselves to think about all the institutions essential to such a world.

The time has come to recognize that good intentions are not enough, to part with sentimental follies, and to expose power-seeking politicians who call the demagoguery of the welfare state democracy. It should be clear that there is no one panacea for the problems of society. No fanatic—no one who would transform the world by hate and revolution—has anything but misery and frustration to offer mankind.

This manifesto is submitted to the thoughtful and concerned men and women of the world urging them to assume the intellectual and moral leadership of mankind in order to replace those who have demonstrated incompetence, lack of vision, greed, bigotry, and brutality.

Humanization and Social Renaissance

A good society cannot be created unless a determining number of the thoughtful and concerned men and women in each country exercise

---

Ralph Borsodi wrote this manifesto in Ambala, Punjab, India in October 1958.

influence and see that power is properly utilized. The process of humanizing individuals and society calls first for reeducation, not for political and economic action. To depend only on new institutions is a mistake. If this mistake is made, the best set of institutions will be perverted. The letter of the new institutions will be honored but the spirit disregarded. The ultimate end will be a repetition of those repeated declines in civilization that dot the tragic pages of history.

For this reason, a program of educational reform as is here presented is absolutely essential.

A New Leadership. The leadership that the priests lost to the warriors, the warriors to the kings, the kings to the business men, the business men to the financiers, and that the financiers are now losing to the politicians, must be assumed by a group that sharply distinguishes between the exercise of influence and the exercise of power. The minority of concerned and thoughtful teachers and writers, of poets and preachers, of artists and scientists, of physicians and lawyers, who constitute the real leadership of any society, must be reborn. They should consecrate themselves to the search and realization of what is true, what is good, what is beautiful.

They must go even further. They must not only seek and create, they must also teach. They must equip those whom they influence with the accumulated knowledge and wisdom of both the East and West, and of the ancient and modern world. They must furnish inspiration, not only instruction. They must motivate those whom they influence to live on a high moral, intellectual, and cultural level. Without such a leadership, no good society and no good life can either be created or maintained.

Academic Autonomy. Universities above all other institutions should be staffed by men and women of quality. But to enable them to furnish unbiased and impartial leadership to individuals and society, the universities must be autonomous—they must be completely free and independent. They must cease being dependent upon government; they must be freed from the necessity of catering to public officials. They must be freed from the dictation of partisan ideologies; of the evangelists of religion; of commercial, industrial, and financial leaders. Academic autonomy is not real unless universities are completely free to seek the truth. Without this freedom, they will omit teaching what is offensive to those who control them; they will warp what they teach so as to please them; they will teach what those upon whom they depend demand of them.

Basic Instruction. Every child must be taught all that is essential to their humanization—a useful craft and the cultivation of the Earth; the practice of domestic arts; to read, write, and use numbers. All must be imbued with the basic virtues—the love of nature, of beauty, and of mankind without regard to race, religion, or nationality. Basic instruction in these matters should begin in the home and continue in the school. No good society can be created without this basic instruction.

Professional Instruction. Instruction to the limit of the interest and capacities of every individual calls for some professional instruction for the more gifted and diligent, in one of the various fields essential to maintaining a genuinely civilized society. Yet specialization should not exclude the *general* education essential to developing each person's whole personality. General education must not merely furnish information, but must imbue individuals with high purposes and values so that professionals and managers do not use their special skills only for their own aggrandizement.

Academic Education. Education is clearly distinguished from instruction. Higher education in liberal arts and the humanities is the right of all exceptionally gifted men and women. Every family and every community should consider it both a privilege and an obligation to enable their gifted sons and daughters to cultivate their talents. Higher education, however, must not produce only scholars and intellectuals, but a class of selfless, inspired, and creative thinkers, scientists, writers, artists, and professional men and women. They must also be imbued with fortitude and courage along with such deep love of humanity as to live, and if necessary sacrifice their lives, for preserving the rights of free persons and the values essential to a good society. Higher education should equip the exceptionally endowed men and women to furnish the wisdom and knowledge for a social renaissance and for the progressive humanization of human kind.

Moral Reeducation. Education at every level must deal with values and purpose. Fallacies in this area must be exposed: moral relativism and modern amoralism; the doctrine that positive law is the only binding law; the theory that all statutory and even constitutional law must be obeyed even in disregard of absolute moral law. The moral law is the natural law, universal and perpetual. Like all natural laws, it must be discovered and constantly and more explicitly formulated. Moral law should, under no circumstance, be confused with mere legislative fiat. The moral law is binding upon all faiths, all nations, all races, all statutes. Legislative acts that disregard it (no matter how enacted nor how powerfully enforced) are null and void.

Teaching moral law should begin in the home and should continue in school. Humanization of education in school and college is essential for the moral reeducation called for here. For millenniums moral education has been warped by priesthoods. As a result, moral education today is full of inappropriate theological injunctions. Moral reeducation calls for separation between metaphysical creed and ethical obligation.

The true first commandment is "Harmony, not discord." This prohibits all dogmatism, fanaticism, persecution. It is binding on all humankind. It enjoins every religion, nation, and race, and every political, social, and economic doctrine, to be tolerant of every person except only the intolerant. "Harmony, not discord" calls for the tolerance of dissent and difference that is essential if the world is to be really free. Discord, with disregard of the rights of others, is the inevitable result of intolerance. Discord is involved when violence is done to individuals by private persons or groups engaged in imposing their intolerance upon them. Mass-discord is involved when mass-violence and mass-killing are indulged in by political or governmental promotion of intolerance. Such intolerance calls for disciplining those who practice it, with essential force, until completely ended. Ostracizing intolerants is recommended.

Discord should not be confused with disturbance. It disturbs mistaken people to learn the truth about their mistaken beliefs, values, activities, and education. But to learn the truth is essential to the humanization of everybody, including those whom it disturbs. Discovering truth is a kind of discipline, and it may be uncomfortable as are most other kinds of discipline. But truth creates a foundation upon which harmony replaces the static acceptance of discordant mistakes. Ralph Waldo Emerson said, "Choose between truth and repose. You can never have both."

There is no *one* final Truth. Rather, *truths* can be distilled about all areas of living—i.e., those formulations of values and facts which (when practiced) result in continuing growth and well-being of persons.

Humanization of the Family System. The family system should be normalized. Archaic patriarchal family systems must be modernized. The disintegrated and atomized modern family must become an organic entity again. For it is the family, not the individual, which is the primary unit of society. And the family's responsibility for its members must be recognized if there is to be any social renaissance. The evidence that establishes the family as the essential nursery of human virtues is overwhelming. This all-important activity, now usurped by the school and the state, must once again be reestablished as the principal function of family life.

Revival of the Small Community. Social and cultural revival of the small community is just as essential as are economic prosperity and political autonomy. Small communities are primarily agricultural for the most part. But if life in them is to be humanized they must be centers of arts and education, as well as of trade, craft, manufacture, and entertainment. Small communities tend to decay if they do not provide all the institutions and enterprises necessary to the basic needs and humane desires of the people who live in them.

The gifted young who have been given the privilege of higher education, perhaps in distant colleges and universities, should be inspired to bring back to the families that have nurtured them, and to the communities in which they have been reared, the skills and good taste that they have been privileged to cultivate.

Regionalism. Not the nation but the region is the true unit of the world. (Cultural nationalism is not to be confused with political nationalism.) The nation-state today is almost always an artificial aggregation of regional cultures. Regional arts should be developed—regional poetry and literature, music and dancing, regional festivals, costumes, architecture. The genius of each region should be encouraged. The present insistence upon standardization of culture and upon the creation of one uniform national or world culture should be arrested.

Pan-Humanism. All human beings, while members of smaller units, are members of humanity. Membership is concurrent in groups of differing area and levels. Real social renaissance for all humankind will not come until every vestige of unilateral and exclusive citizenship in *nations* is abolished and people everywhere recognize that their obligations to humanity are above those of nation-states. Not the nation "right or wrong," but the world, the region, the community, and the family are entitled to claim people's allegiance.

Between the region and the whole world, every social, cultural, economic, and political entity is an arbitrary construct, which should be used only to develop regions more freely on the one hand and the whole world on the other. To whatever extent nation-states now usurp the normal functions (and prevent normal development) of the whole world, they should be abolished.

Political Liberty

Creating a new leadership and reorganizing educational institutions so that humankind may be humanized is the first step in the birth of the sort of world for which human beings are hungering. But more is necessary.

Good intentions and rigorous thinking must be followed by action. The social, economic, and political institutions that inflict economic injustice and interfere with political liberty must be abolished. Those that are imperfect must be reformed, and those that are missing must be created by the *voluntary* activities of individuals and groups, corporations, and cooperatives, and, where necessary, by political action, statutory changes, or constitutional reform.

Human beings are not mere animals. They have, it is true, an inherited, instinctual drive for self-survival (an economic drive). Also in common with animals, they have a sexual drive for self-production. But much higher than these two is the last instinctual drive with which evolution has endowed humankind—the drive for self-expression.

It is for this reason that no political institution can be considered human and properly adapted to the nature of humankind if it in any way infringes upon liberty; if it, even in the slightest, interferes with the conditions necessary to individual self-expression and to the free development of the highest potentialities of being human. Six fundamental political reforms are needed if the new world, now being born, is to better provide for human liberty than the "free" world (even at its best) is providing.

1. *The Obligations and Rights of Human Beings.* Every human being confronts natural obligations—the obligation to respect the person, the possessions, the premises, and the rights of other human beings; the obligation to utter no libels or slanders; the obligation not to interfere in any way with the peaceful religious, political, economic, or social activities of others. Each person has the obligation to protect basic rights and enforce these obligations by the payment of just taxes and by answering every just call of any properly constituted local, regional, or world authority to defend them even at the cost of life and property.

Every human being has certain inalienable rights—to life, to liberty, and to property; the right to defense of his person and property; to sue others (including public officials for compensation for damages inflicted); the right to travel anywhere in the world; to free speech and publication; to peacefully assemble and seek correction of injustices; the right to freedom from search and seizure of himself, his possessions, and his premises. Due process must always be observed—he must be represented by counsel, the judges must be impartial, the same facilities must be furnished for securing witnesses as those enjoyed by the state, and he must be presumed to be innocent until the charges against him are proved beyond reasonable doubt. Every regulation, ordinance, statute, or constitutional provision that violates any of these natural rights—being morally null and void—must be repealed forthwith. The violation of any of these natural rights by any public official constitutes malfeasance, and such public official should be removed for usurpation.

The multiplicity of encroachments on these rights by so-called democratic governments and welfare states must be ended and every encroachment repealed. All dictatorial governments, including those ostensibly set up to promote socialism (called people's democracies), are by their very nature violators of these rights.

2. *Limited Government.* The functions and authority of all government bodies shall be limited to those that are necessary to preserving these rights and to enforcing the fulfillment of these obligations. The exercise of power by a government for any other purpose whatsoever is invalid. Assumption by a government of any function that can be fulfilled by private persons and private enterprises shall constitute usurpation. Any regulation, ordinance, statute, or constitutional provision that legalizes such usurpation shall be treated by all persons as null and void.

3. *Local Autonomy.* No free society (in which people truly participate and so give continuing consent to what government does) can long endure unless the primary political unit (the village, borough, township, commune, canton) is autonomous. The present system by which a centralized state exercises power over local communities or "grants" limited power to them must be ended. Ultimate power is in the people, and they grant specific powers upward to their local community; communities delegate certain powers to county or district; the counties or districts to regional federation; and so on until regional federations in the whole world finally grant specific powers to a world *federation*. It is usurpation for power to descend from a centralized state to the people. Today local autonomy calls for political decentralization.

4. *Federation.* Human history has demonstrated that democracy (real participation of the people in government) is possible only in relatively small local communities. In all larger units of government, participation by the people becomes merely formal. All such larger units of government become representative or "republican" in form.

Representation calls for federation (not union) of all units of government larger than the local community. Federation must therefore be substituted for the present oligarchical or autocratic organization of all larger units of government, beginning with the county or district, and ending with the world. Not national union, but regional federation—not world union but world federation—is called for. Federation calls for a multiplicity of government units, each with specific functions delegated to it by the smaller units that constitute it, until at the base, ultimate, residuary powers are exercised by the people in their own autonomous communities.

My strong condemnation of nationalism is accompanied by a proposal for a world authority federally organized and strong enough to maintain international peace. (Until such a world authority is a reality, it could not be expected that nations would surrender their sovereignty.) The United Nations as it is now organized violates the basic principles of federation. In spite of the passionate devotion of those who believe in it, the United Nations is a fraud perpetrated by the great powers upon a peace-hungry world. As now organized, the United Nations pretends to, but cannot, maintain world peace.

5. *Concurrent Jurisdiction.* Implicit in the two great principles of autonomy and federation is the principle of concurrent jurisdiction. Since every unit of government (from the local community to the world federation) should have only *specific and limited* powers, and since those powers entrusted to larger units of government must be exercised within the areas (and over the people in) the smaller units, jurisdiction must be concurrent—not exclusive or absolute.

This principle of concurrent jurisdiction applies to all levels of government because no federated unit of government can fulfill its specific functions if its jurisdiction is limited by the government of any region in which it has to operate. Concurrent jurisdiction is essential if effective federal action is not to be frustrated and conditions result in further centralization of power rather than limiting government.

6. *Consent of the Governed by Self-Determination.* People of every region have a basic political right to live under a government that governs with their consent. Yet hundreds of millions of people today are governed in violation of this essential human right. Liberty and democracy are mocked by this tragic fact. Millions of people are governed by "people's democracies" which in reality are Communist dictatorships. Other millions are ruled by combined native and foreign oligarchies under the military power of great nations. Millions of colonies are governed despotically by governments that operate more "democratically" at home. Millions more in Asia and Latin America are governed by military or political dictators and oligarchies. Tragically, dissenting minorities in these despotisms are accorded inhuman treatment.

World-wide autonomy and federation are ultimately the answers to these problems. Democracy breaks down and falls into the hands of political oligarchies when the units of government are large. In such cases, nations feel justified in intervening. An adequate world federation is needed as an impartial trustee to assist formation of stable and free governments for the millions now enslaved or subjected to foreign and dictatorial rule not of their own choosing.

Economic Justice

If the whole world is to be made free, and the peoples of the so-called free world made completely free, justice and not equality must be the aim of the economic order. It is not true that economic equality must be *imposed* by government upon humankind, in order to abolish poverty. Prosperity is highest where political tyranny and economic injustice are lowest. Poverty, on the other hand, continues in proportion as equality is imposed.

Justice is in accord with nature's laws and should be the aim of all effort, including legal effort. Legalized equality is an attempt to abrogate nature's laws. Justice provides economic incentives; enforced equality destroys them.

Is it justice for the slack and shiftless laborer to receive the same wage as the one who works diligently and efficiently? Is it justice to pay the person who has devoted years of life to training the same as the person who has cultivated no skill and has been indifferent to training and education? Is it justice to reward the person who has been thrifty, invested savings productively, taken risks and responsibilities in conducting an enterprise, the same as the person who spends all his earnings, saves and invests nothing, risks nothing and takes on no responsibility of any kind?

Justice is the expression of the moral law. Enforced equality is a form of compulsory charity. Charity to the victims of unavoidable misfortune is a human obligation. But this is a voluntary, individual (and not a political) obligation.

A principle to govern a just and moral economic order is: "to each contributor in proportion to his contribution"—to labor, capital, industry, agriculture, and management—to each what each contributes to the production of wealth. To establish this principle in the new world aborning, seven fundamental reforms of the present economic order are essential.

1. *Free Enterprise.* No truly just social system is possible if freedom to

embark upon enterprise is denied or curtailed. Freedom is not possible if special privileges are granted to one enterprise that handicap others, or if freedom to work (or employ any individual) is infringed by laws of any kind. Political freedom is mocked when economic freedom is curtailed. Equality *of opportunity* is essential to insure full use of capital and labor, to furnish incentive and encourage initiative, and to assure justice in the division of wealth between capital and labor and between industry and agriculture. We must abolish all special privileges, differential tariffs, subsidies, quotas, licenses, limited liability corporations, and all cartels or monopolies (particularly in banking) in the private sector of the economy.

Today, *predatory* competition is permitted and encouraged by the granting of special privileges to particular persons, companies, and classes. Until this is ended there can be no real free market, no *fraternal* competition in establishing wages and prices, no just return to agriculture and other producers of basic raw materials.

The cure for what is wrong in the so-called free world today is not to confer offsetting special privileges (which was begun during the 1930s under the Franklin Roosevelt administration). The cure is to repeal existing special privileges.

Among the most crucial and least understood special privileges are those granted to corporations. Three of these are outstandingly unjust: (1) limited liability, (2) nonassessibility of stockholders of corporations, and (3) exemption of directors and officers for liability for misfeasance, nonfeasance, and malfeasance. Such special privileges to corporations have inhibited the growth of cooperative enterprises. One responsibility of the new leadership is to fire the imagination, stimulate the organization, and train management of cooperatives so that cooperatives develop where the nature of the enterprise calls for cooperation.

This occurred in Denmark and in other countries where cooperation flourishes. Leaders inspired by the Danish folk schools transformed the economic order of Denmark. A veritable revolution took place slowly under the initiative of men and women whom I regard as consecrated members of the new leadership.

The terrible handicaps under which proprietary enterprise in America operates can be corrected. The existing land tenure can be changed to one that is genuinely just. The dishonest money system can become stable. The present imperfect market system can be free—and competition can work so that prices, wages, rent, interest, and profits are fair and just. This calls for new leadership and reeducation.

Free enterprise in a free economic order is not of one kind (private) only. It is of three totally different kinds: (1) proprietary, (2) corporate, and (3) cooperative. All three of these spontaneously arise and progress unless they are interfered with by the granting of special privileges to one and the imposition of handicaps upon others.

2. *Prices in a Complex Industrial System.* Only through a free market can prices be justly established and economic activities effectively regulated. This calls for each producer producing his best, but in such a market, competition must be fraternal. In a free market, cooperation between buyers and sellers establishes prices that are just. Fraternal competition must replace all the forms of predatory competition that we mistakenly accept or excuse in the present capitalistic order. To create a truly free market, all regulation and interference by government of prices, wages, rent, interest, and profits must be abolished. The market can justly regulate them in accord with the law of supply and demand.

3. *Mutualization.* No just society is possible unless it is recognized that not two but three distinct sectors exist in every economy: (1) the naturally private, (2) the naturally monopolistic, and (3) the naturally public. All natural monopolies—railroads, power companies, water services, gas companies, pipelines, telegraph and telephone systems, irrigation districts, banks of issue—must be mutualized (owned and operated in the interests of those who use them). By rebating all surplus earnings pro rata to users, they insure that their services are furnished at cost and that no profits are appropriated by private interests or exploited by the government.

4. *Free Trade.* All differential and so-called protective tariffs must be abolished, and national boundaries in essence must be abolished. National boundaries must cease being economic barriers. They should be reduced to administrative conveniences. Basically all peoples, all creeds, all races have the human right to trade freely with one another. *If free trade is good within a country, free trade is good between countries.* Customs guards must be ended and recognition given to the fact that all mankind belongs to one human race, if a free and just economic order is to replace the capitalistic and socialistic economies of today.

5. *Free Banking: Honest Currency; Stable Money.* Government control and regulation of banks—private, commercial, and mutual—must be ended. Banks should be free to provide credit as needed by all legitimate borrowers. The natural monopoly of issue of legal-tender currency should be restricted to cooperatively-organized reserve banks. Banking is a

profession, not a business. Banks that create credit and issue money should be cooperative and not commercial enterprises.

Nothing has done more to discredit capitalism or to destroy faith in a free economy than the use of a banking system for private aggrandizement, and the use of the money system for meeting the deficits of government. The gross immorality of debauching the currency must be ended. The business cycle with its boom and bust is a monetary phenomenon. There are no unsolved technical difficulties in creating a stable and honest unit of currency.

6. *Free Access to the Possession of Land.* A just system of land tenure is essential to ending employment, wage-slavery, and landowners' exploitation of farmers. By arranging equality of access to land for everyone, laborers and tenants will have the alternative of going to the land and producing on their own. This adds to their bargaining power in dealing with employers and landowners. It is their alternative to accepting unjust wages or payment of excessive rent to landowners.

All the natural resources of the earth—the land, the forests, the oil, the minerals, and the waters—are the gift of nature to all humankind. No title to absolute ownership of any part of the Earth can be traced back to a deed issued by the creator of the Earth. All natural resources are by their nature *trusterty, not property.* Land should be privately *possessed* (not owned to buy and sell) to be used for incentive to its fullest and most efficient use. But the unearned increment (the ground rent and the mineral royalties), instead of being privately appropriated, should be used instead of taxes to pay for the necessary services provided by the community.

Apologists for capitalism defend private property in land. They defend speculation in land. Such insistence has hopelessly identified capitalism with the injustices of the present land-tenure system in the "free" world. Communist alternatives—nationalization and collectivization of land—can be avoided. A new system of land tenure can be based on the ethical principles of Mencius in China and Henry George in America.

7. *Freedom of Possession.* Title to property can originate legitimately in one way—by its production. Once created in this way, title to it can be transferred or exchanged for other property, the ownership of which has come into existence the same way. The law of property in a free world must be revised so as to distinguish not only between what is mine and what is yours, but also between them and what is ours. Both property and trusterty exist. Community collection of what is "ours"—the ground rent

of natural resources—would be in the direction of justice. Other taxes could be eliminated as limited government replaces unlimited government and as world federation replaces national efforts for defense.

A New Leadership

An ideological vacuum exists in the free world and in the military and Communist dictatorships of the world. The world has lost its bearings. People are disillusioned with mass poverty, government support, exploitation, rural decay, urban blight, imperialism, and militarism. They languish in the denial of liberty. Many people are sick even of prosperity in which the human spirit is alienated. Because of the scientific revolution, many are ready to abandon the dogmatisms of religion. They are ready to turn from demagogues and nationalism. They are looking for something fresh and new, something to give purpose and meaning worthy of the human spirit.

Promises are made to abolish all existing evils with the panacea of the state—organized force and compulsion. Masses have been, and are being, dazzled by these golden promises. What do the active leaders of the free world have to offer? In sum, they offer continuance of what we now have in the so-called democratic world. But this is what most of mankind has already subconsciously rejected. This is the ideological vacuum that gives to the statists their opportunity. But this rejection is what also affords opportunity to a new leadership to provide truly human solutions.

A new leadership faces a real difficulty—one they do not welcome and confront courageously. Our difficulty is that *we cannot create a good world quickly.*

But if the program presented is adequate; if it deals with the roots of our social and human weakness, then every year there will be improvements—and they will accumulate geometrically. But to reach the hard-core common sense of people, to enlist the enthusiastic support of intelligent men and women, the program must be explicit. It must be comprehensive and persuasively presented. And it must be promoted by selfless leaders who do not discredit themselves by apologizing for the evils of the present order.

Neither capitalism as it exists in the so-called free nations nor socialism in the so-called welfare states, nor Communism in the so-called people's democracies are adequate social orders. Social renaissance calls for abandonment of socialism and Communism and transforming capitalism into a free and just economic order.

No such changes in economic institutions of both democratic and dictatorial countries are possible without reeducation and humanization of at least a determining number of men and women in the world. Drastic political and economic changes are not enough. In the final analysis, if humankind is to be saved from a mechanical and materialistic barbarism, if people are to be taught to live rationally, lovingly, and humanely, the educators of mankind must furnish the leadership that the crisis calls for. *Then* men and women in every race and country can create liberty and justice for all humanity.

No words can make clear that none of the radical changes in the political and economic institutions of the world here called for will, by themselves, create a good society. No genuinely good society or good life for individuals is possible without radical changes in the prevailing system of education throughout the world.

If our inner spirits are neglected; if moral values are missing from education; if no love of liberty, beauty, truth, and justice is instilled in human beings; if creative faculties are dulled in the home, schools, recreation, and work—the notion that a perfect set of institutions will produce a good society and a good way of life is fantastic. If this mistake is made, the best set of institutions will be perverted, and the ultimate end will be another decline in civilization.

Bibliography

ORGANIZATIONS

The American Institute of
Cooperation
1800 Massachusetts Ave., N.W.
Washington, D.C. 20036

Community Service, Inc.
Box 243
Yellow Springs, Ohio 45387

Cooperative League of the U.S.A.
1828 L St., N.W.
Washington, D.C. 20036

The Henry George School of Social
Science and
The Robert Schalkenbach Foundation
5 East 44th St.
New York, N.Y. 10017

Institute for Community Economics
120 Boylston St.
Boston, Mass. 01505

Ken Kern Enterprises
P.O. Box 550
Oakhurst, Calif. 93644

Movement for a New Society
1006 South 46th St.
Philadelphia, Pa. 19143

New World Alliance
733 15th St., N.W. #1131
Washington, D.C. 20005

The School of Living
P.O. Box 3233
York, Pa. 17402

MAGAZINES

CoEvolution Quarterly
(quarterly, $14.00)
Box 428
Sausalito, Calif. 94965

Green Revolution
(bimonthly, $8.00)
The School of Living
P.O. Box 3233
York, Pa. 17402

In Business
(bimonthly, $14.00)
Box 323
18 South Seventh St.
Emmaus, Pa. 18049

Manas
(weekly, $10.00)
P.O. Box 32112
Los Angeles, Calif. 90032

Mother Earth News
(bimonthly, $15.00)
P.O. Box 70
Hendersonville, N.C. 28739

New Age Magazine
(monthly, $15.00)
Box 1200
Allston, Mass. 02134

New Shelter
(9 times per year, $10.00)
33 East Minor St.
Emmaus, Pa. 18049

Organic Gardening
(monthly, $11.00)
33 East Minor St.
Emmaus, Pa. 18049

Prevention
(monthly, $10.97)
33 East Minor St.
Emmaus, Pa. 18049

The Storm! A Journal of Free Spirits
(5 issues for $4.00; 1 issue for $1.00)

227 Columbus Ave. #2E
New York, N.Y. 10023

Survival Tomorrow
(monthly, $60.00)
901 North Washington St.
Alexandria, Va. 22314

BOOKS

ANARCHISM

De Leon, David. *The American as Anarchist.* Baltimore: Johns Hopkins University Press, 1978.

Martin, James J. *Men Against the State: The Expositors of Individualist Anarchism in America.* Colorado Springs, Colo.: Ralph Myles, 1970.

Oppenheimer, Franz. *The State.* New York: Free Life Editions, 1975.

Spooner, Lysander. *No Treason.* Colorado Springs, Colo.: Ralph Myles, 1966.

Tucker, Benjamin R. *Instead of a Book: By a Man Too Busy to Write One, a Fragmentary Exposition of Philosophical Anarchism.* New York: Arno Press, 1972.

COOPERATIVES

Dodge, Philip J. *People Help Themselves Through Cooperatives.* New York: AMS Press, 1973.

Dublin, Jack. *Credit Unions: Theory and Practice.* Detroit: Wayne State University Press, 1971.

Liblit, Jerome. *Housing the Cooperative Way: Selected Readings.* New York: Cyrco Press, n.d.

Voorhis, Horace J. *American Cooperatives.* Westport, Conn.: Greenwood, 1974.

Warbasse, James Peter. *Consumer Cooperation.* New York: Consumers Cooperative Publishing Association, 1969.

LAND AND HENRY GEORGE

Barnes, Peter. *The People's Land.* Emmaus, Pa.: Rodale, 1975.

Bowen, Elizabeth, and George Rushby. *Economics Simplified.* New York: Robert Schalkenbach Foundation, 1942.

George, Henry. *The Land for the People.* New York: Robert Schalkenbach Foundation, 1975.

George, Henry. *Progress and Poverty.* New York: Robert Schalkenbach Foundation, 1978.

Sirofani, Robert. *Who Owns the Earth? What Is It Worth?* San Francisco: Henry George School, 1981.
Swann, Robert. *The Community Land Trust: A New Land Tenure for America.* Boston: Institute for Community Economics, 1972.

BOOKS BY RALPH BORSODI

Education and Living. Old Greenwich, Conn.: Devin-Adair, 1948.
Flight from the City. New York: Harper & Row, 1972.
Let's Stop Inflation. Available from the School of Living.
Seventeen Problems of Man and Society. Anand, India: Charotar Book Stall, 1968.
This Ugly Civilization. Philadelphia: Porcupine Press, 1975.

NUTRITION, SOIL, AND HEALTH

Balfour, Lady Eve. *The Living Soil and the Haughley Experiment.* New York: Universe Books, 1976.
Carson, Rachel. *The Silent Spring.* Boston: Houghton Mifflin, 1962.
Darwin, Charles. *Darwin on Humus and the Earth Worm: The Formation of Vegetable Mold* (1892). Ontario, Calif.: Bookworm Publishing Co., 1976.
Davis, Adelle. *Let's Cook It Right.* New York: New American Library, 1970.
———. *Let's Eat Right to Keep Fit.* New York: New American Library, 1970.
———. *Let's Get Well.* New York: New American Library, 1972.
———. *Let's Stay Healthy: A Guide to Lifelong Nutrition.* Edited and expanded by Ann Gildroy. New York: Harcourt Brace Jovanovich, 1981.
Hastings, Arthur, James Fadiman, and James Gordon, eds. *Health for the Whole Person.* Boulder, Colo.: Westview Press, 1980.
King, F. H. *Farmers for Forty Centuries* (1911). Emmaus, Pa.: Rodale Press, 1973.
Lappé, Frances Moore. *Diet for a Small Planet.* New York: Ballantine, 1975.
———. *Food First.* New York: Ballantine, 1979.
McLaughlin, Terence. *If You Like It, Don't Eat It: Dietary Fads and Fancies.* New York: Universe Books, 1978.
Nutrition Search, Inc. *Nutrition Almanac.* New York: McGraw-Hill, 1973.
Price, Weston A. *Nutrition and Physical Degeneration.* La Mesa, Calif.: Price-Pottenger Nutrition Foundation, 1977.
Tilden, John. *Toxemia, the Basic Cause of Disease.* Chicago: Natural Hygiene Press, 1974.
Wrench, G. T. *The Wheel of Health: The Sources of Long Life and Health Among the Hunza.* New York: Schocken, 1972.

COMMUNITY

Berger, Peter L., and Richard J. Neuhaus. *To Empower People.* Washington: American Enterprise Institute, 1977.

French, David and Elena. *Working Communally.* New York: Russell Sage, 1975.
Goodman, Paul and Percival. *Communities: Means of Livelihood and Ways of Life.* New York: Random House, 1960.
Hess, Karl. *Community Technology.* New York: Harper & Row, 1979.
Jordan, Clarence. *The Cotton Patch Evidence.* Chicago: Follett, 1973.
Kotler, Milton. *Neighborhood Government.* Indianapolis: Bobbs-Merrill, 1969.
Kriyananda, Swami. *Cooperative Communities: How to Start Them, and Why.* Nevada City, Calif.: Ananda, 1968.
Kropotkin, Peter. *Mutual Aid.* New York: New York University Press, 1972.
Morgan, Arthur E. *The Community of the Future.* Yellow Springs, Ohio: Community Service, 1957.
————. *The Long Road.* Yellow Springs, Ohio: Community Service, 1936.
Morris, David, and Karl Hess. *Neighborhood Power.* Boston: Beacon Press, 1975.
Rivers, Patrick. *The Survivalists.* New York: Universe Books, 1975.
Skinner, B. F. *Walden Two* (1948). New York: Macmillan, 1969.
Van Dresser, Peter. *Landscape for Humans.* Santa Fe, N.M.: The Lightning Tree, 1972.

HOMESTEADING

Cobbett, William. *Cottage Economy.* New York: Kelley, 1970.
Freed, Dolly. *Possum Living: How to Live Without a Job and with Almost No Money.* New York: Universe Books, 1978.
Gwinn, Ralph, and Frank Fritts. *Fifth Avenue to Farm: A Biological Approach to the Problem of the Survival of Our Civilization.* New York: Harper, 1938.
Hall, Bolton. *A Little Land and a Living.* New York: Arcadia, 1908.
Loomis, Mildred J. *Go Ahead and Live.* New Canaan, Conn.: Keats, 1972.
Nearing, Helen and Scott. *Living the Good Life.* New York: Schocken, 1970.
Rivers, Patrick. *The Survivalists.* New York: Universe Books, 1975.
Rodale, Robert. *Sane Living in a Mad World.* Emmaus, Pa.: Rodale, 1972.
Seymour, John and Sally. *Farming and Self-Sufficiency.* New York: Schocken, 1976.
Tobe, John. *Living on the Land.* Ontario, Calif.: Provoker Press, 1970.
Vivian, John. *The Manual of Practical Homesteading.* Emmaus, Pa.: Rodale, 1975.
Wend, Milton. *How to Live in the Country without Farming: Planning and Establishing a Productive Country House.* Garden City, N.Y.: Doubleday, Doran, 1944.

HOME BUILDING

Burns, Scott. *Home, Inc.* New York: Doubleday, 1975.
Clarke, Robin. *Building for Self-Sufficiency.* New York: Universe Books, 1977.
Kern, Ken. *The Owner-Built Home* (1955). New York: Scribner, 1975.
————. *The Owner-Built Homestead* (1958). New York: Scribner, 1975.
————. *Stone Masonry: Owner-Builder's Guide No. 1.* New York: Scribner, 1977.

Thnallon, Rob, and Ted Kogan. *The Code: The Politics of Building Your Own Home.* New York: Scribner, 1977.

Van Dresser, Peter. *Homegrown Sundwellings.* Santa Fe, N.M.: The Lightning Tree, 1977.

Wright, Frank Lloyd. *The Natural House.* New York: Horizon, 1954.

MONEY

Brandeis, Louis D. *Other People's Money* (1932). New York: Kelley, 1971.

Dahlberg, Arthur. *How to Save Free Enterprise.* Old Greenwich, Conn.: Devin-Adair, 1975.

Fisher, Irving. *Mathematical Investigations into the Theory of Value and Prices* (1892). New York: Kelley, 1965.

Gesell, Silvio. *The New Economic Order.* New York: Gordon Press, n.d.

Soddy, Frederick. *The Role of Money.* New York: Gordon Press, 1976.

PERSONAL GROWTH

Loomis, Mildred J. *Evolving for Social Change.* Available from the School of Living.

Maddaloni, Arnold. *To Be Fully Alive.* New York: Horizon, 1964.

Marks, Clear. *Friendly Shared Powers.* San Diego, Calif.: Clear Marks, 1979.

Maslow, Abraham H. *The Further Reaches of Human Nature.* New York: Viking, 1971.

Pearce, Joseph Chilton. *Magical Child.* New York: Dutton, 1977.

Roszak, Theodore. *Person-Planet.* New York: Doubleday, 1979.

Schroeder, Theodore. *How Do You Think.* Available from the School of Living.

Spring, Joel. *A Primer of Libertarian Education.* New York: Free Life Editions, 1975.

Werkheiser, Don. *Growing into an Adult.* Available from the School of Living.

DECENTRALISM

Ellul, Jacques. *Technological Society.* New York: Random House, 1967.

Freed, Dolly. *Possum Living: How to Live Well Without a Job and with Almost No Money.* New York: Universe Books, 1978.

Hawken, Paul. *The Magic of Findhorn.* New York: Harper & Row, 1975.

Henderson, Hazel. *Creating Alternative Futures.* New York: Berkeley Press, 1978.

Lippmann, Walter. *The Good Society.* Westport, Conn.: Greenwood, 1973.

Morgan, Arthur E. *Industries for Small Communities.* Yellow Springs, Ohio: Community Service, 1953.

Mumford, Lewis. *Technics and Civilization.* New York: Harcourt Brace Jovanovich, 1963.

Sale, Kirkpatrick. *Human Scale*. New York: Coward, McCann & Geohegan, 1980.

Satin, Mark. *New Age Politics*. New York: Dell, 1979.

Schumacher, E. F. *Small is Beautiful*. New York: Harper & Row, 1973.

Shortney, John Ransom. *How to Live on Nothing*. New York: Simon and Schuster, 1968.

Thoreau, Henry David. *Walden and Civil Disobedience*. New York: NAL, 1973.

Index